THE ASTROLOGY ALMANAC

2024

EMMA HOWARTH

ILLUSTRATED BY

KATARINA SAMOHIN

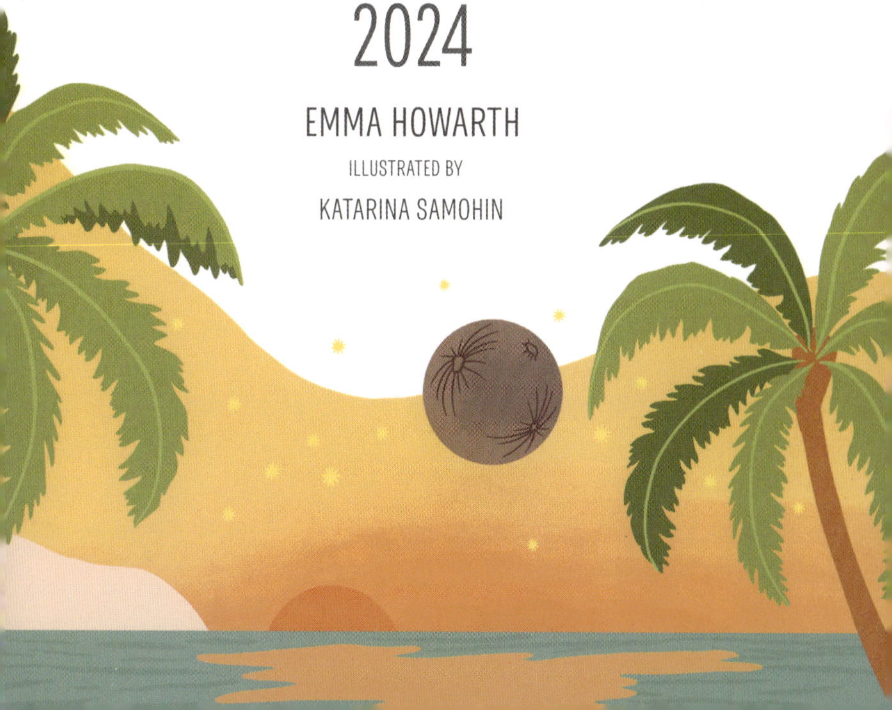

CONTENTS

INTRODUCTION 4

HOW TO USE THIS BOOK 5

YOUR BIRTH CHART 6

READ FOR YOUR RISING SIGN 7

THE BIG THREE 8

THE PLANETS

The Personal Planets 10

The Social Planets 14

The Generational Planets 18

ASTROLOGICAL SEASONS OF 2024 22

WHEEL OF THE YEAR 2024 23

MOONS OF 2024 24

RETROGRADES OF 2024 25

THE MODALITIES 26

THE ELEMENTS 27

♑ JANUARY 28

♒ FEBRUARY 46

♓ MARCH 60

♈ APRIL 80

♉ MAY 98

♊ JUNE 114

♋ JULY 132

♌ AUGUST 146

♍ SEPTEMBER 160

♎ OCTOBER 174

♏ NOVEMBER 188

♐ DECEMBER 202

DIVE DEEPER

The Houses 218
Moon Phases 220
Aspects 221
More, More, More 221

About the Author and Illustrator 222

Acknowledgements 223

INTRODUCTION

Life feels more magical when you're gazing at the stars – and doubling down on that magic is easy when you begin to understand them. The more hectic modern life becomes, the more many of us feel drawn to the stories of the zodiac, the mysteries of the moon and the shifting cosmic weather. Played out in newspaper headlines about super moons, collective groans about Mercury retrograde and endless zodiac jewellery collections, astrology is having a moment. And with this *Astrology Almanac 2024* as your guide, you'll soon be having one too.

Within these pages you'll find everything you need to become the oracle of your social circle for the year ahead. Want to know when the next new moon is? Or which planet's retrograde is messing with your head right now? Wondering what Capricorn season is all about? Or how to charm the Leo you met on the beach this summer? Maybe you just want to know why everyone on your Instagram feed is banging on about eclipse season?

We've got you covered, and then some. Take a trip through the astrological seasons from January to December, flick through to read up on your favourite signs and seek solace in guidance from the stars. Whether you're already obsessed with astrology or just getting started, you'll find plenty within these pages to engage, entice and ignite your cosmic intuition.

Magic awaits.

HOW TO USE THIS BOOK

Ready for some magical cosmic reveals? You've come to the right place. This almanac will take you on an astrological journey through the year from January to December, but it can be used in many different ways:

- ★ You can take it a month at a time, savouring the flavour of each zodiac season as it happens.
- ★ You can dip in and out of chapters to discover different astrological signs and what makes you, your friends or a love interest tick.
- ★ You can use it to prepare for the new moons, full moons and eclipses of 2024.
- ★ You can read about the themes that lie ahead for your sign as the astro weather changes each month.
- ★ You can quickly check what planets are currently in retrograde when everything feels crazy in your world.
- ★ And you can read for your sun, moon or rising sign (see p8–9) depending on what kind of insights you need at any given moment.

This book takes a northern hemisphere perspective on the seasons, so if you're reading from the southern hemisphere you may need to switch summer for winter in your mind! The astrological vibes still apply.

Ready to explore the cosmos?

Let's do this.

We've kept this almanac as beginner friendly as possible. If you discover a passion for astrology within these pages and want to know more, there is plenty to learn and discover. See 'Dive Deeper' on p218–221.

YOUR BIRTH CHART

Your birth chart is a snapshot of the sky at the moment you were born and reveals all sorts of cosmic insights into what makes you tick. All you need to discover it is your date, time and place of birth, and access to one of the many free chart generators available online. Good options include astro.com, astro-seek.com and, if you prefer an app, Chani Nicholas's 'Chani' app. I prefer to use a whole sign house system so if you'd like to do the same, select this option in settings (Chani's app uses this system automatically).

There's a lot going on in a birth chart so it can look confusing at first, but gathering the top line information you need to understand yourself and those around you better is fairly simple. Once you know your sun, moon, rising and planetary signs you'll have a much fuller picture of who you are astrologically. Dive deeper (with the help of an astrologer or by learning more about houses, aspects and transits) and you'll discover this very personal cosmic roadmap can help you understand - and even predict - your life, purpose, hopes, dreams and desires.

You don't need to understand your birth chart in great depth to use this book. We've deliberately made this almanac as accessible and straightforward as possible. You will be able to use and enjoy this book if all you know is your sun sign but you may find you get another level of insight once you know your moon, rising and other signs.

Let this be the beginning of a magical astrological journey into the star-studded story of you.

READ FOR YOUR RISING SIGN

Your star sign (or sun sign) is just one part of your astrological profile. Discover your birth chart and you'll find that you also have a moon sign, a Venus sign and a rising sign, among many others. Of all of these signs, your rising sign is the most personal - reflecting your date, time and place of birth - and reveals your public self, how you show up in the world and the first impressions you make on others.

Many people find they relate to their rising sign more than their sun sign and, as far as horoscopes are concerned, once you start reading for your rising sign, we're pretty sure you won't want to stop.

Your rising sign is the sign that was emerging over the eastern horizon at the time of your birth. It's the sign that rules your 1st House (one of the twelve houses of your birth chart, see p218–19), kicking off your entire astrological profile. Basically, if you read the horoscope for your rising sign, it tends to feel more in line with what's going on in your life because it matches up with your birth chart.

That doesn't mean you need to ditch your sun sign, though. Sun signs are an important part of who we are but adding your rising sign to the astro remit offers some seriously fascinating insights. Try it for yourself as you work your way through this book and see how it pans out. You can even try reading for your moon sign too, especially if you're seeking insights into your emotional life.

Rising signs change every couple of hours so you need an accurate birth time to discover yours. This particular piece of cosmic info is a spookily accurate game-changer.

THE BIG THREE

Sun signs might get all the attention but there's so much more to astrology than horoscopes. If you want to understand your cosmic makeup better, a great start is your astrological 'big three'. Your sun, moon and rising sign reveal magical insights into how you think, feel and show up in the world. Try reading the insights for these as well as your sun sign as you work your way through this book.

SUN SIGN

Your core self

This is the big one. Your sun sign reveals the sign the sun was in at the time of your birth. It's the sign most of us already know and connect with in some way, the sign you scan for when you read horoscopes and possibly even use as a handy excuse for your shortcomings... It's not your fault you slept through your alarm, it's your Pisces sun!

CHANGES Every thirty days.

REVEALS Who you are. What makes you tick. Your core values. Your personality and sense of self. Your motivations and innate gifts.

MOON SIGN

Your inner self

Your moon sign tells you which constellation the moon was in at the time of your birth. The moon is associated with feelings and emotions, and your moon sign reveals the side of yourself you don't show to others so readily.

CHANGES Every two and a half days.

REVEALS Your inner self. Your emotional side. What you need to feel secure. Your private longings, fears and desires.

RISING SIGN

Your public self

Your rising sign is the constellation that was on the eastern horizon at the moment of your birth. Of all the astrological placements, this one is the most personal and requires an accurate date, time and place of birth.

CHANGES Every two hours.

REVEALS Your public self. The first impression you make on people. The way you look and present yourself to the world.

YOUR BIG THREE AT A GLANCE

SIGN	SUN	MOON	RISING
ARIES ♈	A rebel	who needs to win	and isn't afraid to take risks
TAURUS ♉	A connoisseur	who isn't in a hurry	and loves the finer things in life
GEMINI ♊	A charmer	who wants to talk	and has endless bright ideas
CANCER ♋	A homebody	who craves stability	and loves so hard it hurts
LEO ♌	A show-off	who needs attention	and always buys the first round
VIRGO ♍	A grafter	who can solve any problem	and loves a five-year plan
LIBRA ♎	A peace-seeker	who just can't choose	and wants everyone to be happy
SCORPIO ♏	A mystic	who craves connection	and doesn't let people in easily
SAGITTARIUS ♐	A globetrotter	who finds life fascinating	and can't wait to start an adventure
CAPRICORN ♑	A CEO	who aims high	and makes it all look easy
AQUARIUS ♒	A free spirit	who wants to save the world	and loves their independence
PISCES ♓	A dreamer	who feels everything deeply	and can make magic happen

THE PLANETS:
THE PERSONAL PLANETS

If the 'big three' - sun, moon and rising signs - represent who we are, then the personal planets (or inner planets) show how we move through life here on Earth. The placements of Mercury, Venus and Mars in your chart (see p6) offer cosmic insight into the way you think, learn, communicate, love and make things happen. These planets move fairly swiftly through the zodiac - unless they're retrograde when they spend longer in a sign - so we feel the influence of each energy shift as we move through the year. Read on for insights into the impact of these cosmic shifts and what the position of these planets in your birth chart might reveal for you.

The tables on the following pages focus on just one element of each planet for a fun snapshot of personal insight. Dive deeper into each sign and you'll find there's much more to discover.

MERCURY

THE MESSENGER – RULER OF GEMINI & VIRGO

Mercury is primarily associated with the mind. Its position at the time of your birth reveals how you make decisions, make progress, learn and communicate with others. See the table opposite for how this might affect your communication style.

- ★ TIME SPENT IN EACH SIGN Two to three weeks.
- ★ RETROGRADES Usually three times a year.
- ★ COSMIC IMPACT As Mercury moves through the signs - and retrogrades three times a year - we feel shifts in the way life moves forwards for us. When Mercury is in Virgo, creating efficient systems to streamline our lives feels easier, and when Mercury is in Libra our focus might shift to communicating better in our relationships or finding more work-life balance.

YOUR MERCURY SIGN & COMMUNICATION

MERCURY IN		YOUR COMMUNICATION STYLE
ARIES	♈	Direct, original, snappy, cutting at times
TAURUS	♉	Thoughtful, sensible, sometimes overly rigid and tunnel-visioned
GEMINI	♊	Gossipy, quick-witted, incredibly open-minded
CANCER	♋	Intense, emotional, slow to open up
LEO	♌	Entertaining, heartfelt, enthusiastic
VIRGO	♍	Considered, pragmatic, chooses words with care
LIBRA	♎	Charming, polite, more focused on listening than talking
SCORPIO	♏	Intuitive, secretive, has a powerful ability to cut others down to size
SAGITTARIUS	♐	Brutally honest, inspiring, argumentative, genuinely interested
CAPRICORN	♑	Practical, strategic, one eye always on the prize
AQUARIUS	♒	Out there, easily bored, detached, unconventional in ideas and approach
PISCES	♓	Expressive, intuitive, emotional, poetic

VENUS

THE LOVER – RULER OF TAURUS & LIBRA

The planet of love and beauty is associated with style, pleasure and romance. Its position in our charts impacts our approach to love and relationships, the way we find pleasure in life and how we express ourselves through personal style. See the table below to discover what your Venus sign reveals about your love vibe.

- ★ TIME SPENT IN EACH SIGN Around thirty days.
- ★ RETROGRADES Every eighteen months (no retrograde in 2024).
- ★ COSMIC IMPACT As Venus moves through the signs we may feel a shift in the ways we express and receive love. When Venus is in Leo love feels dramatic and intense but when Venus moves into Virgo we might feel moved to raise our standards and take our relationships more seriously.

YOUR VENUS SIGN & LOVE

VENUS IN		YOUR LOVE VIBE
ARIES	♈	Assertive, demanding, not into playing games
TAURUS	♉	Slow-paced, seductive, into old-fashioned romance
GEMINI	♊	Flirtatious, easily bored, loves a chat-up line
CANCER	♋	Romantic, nurturing, ready to commit
LEO	♌	Devoted, loyal, a fan of the chase
VIRGO	♍	Practical, discerning, needs to know where it's headed
LIBRA	♎	Committed, romantic, will suffer to keep the peace
SCORPIO	♏	Magnetic, intense, seeking deep connection
SAGITTARIUS	♐	Adventurous, easy-going, will travel for action
CAPRICORN	♑	Serious, committed, ready to be part of a power couple
AQUARIUS	♒	Alternative, independent, will not be tied down
PISCES	♓	Dreamy, sensitive, all about fantasy

MARS

THE WARRIOR – RULER OF ARIES & SCORPIO (CO-RULER)

Mars is associated with passion, sexual attraction, energy, goals and action. Its position in our charts reveals what motivates us, how we gather our energy and who we attract and find attractive. See the table below to reveal how your Mars sign might impact the way you go after a goal.

- ★ TIME SPENT IN EACH SIGN Around two months.
- ★ RETROGRADES Every two years.
- ★ COSMIC IMPACT As Mars moves through the signs our ability to get things done changes. When Mars is in Aries we might be more inclined towards spontaneous plans and direct action, whereas Mars in Taurus plays the long game, slowly moving towards an end result.

YOUR MARS SIGN & GOALS

MARS IN		HOW YOU GO AFTER A GOAL
ARIES	♈	Quickly, impulsively and without thinking it through
TAURUS	♉	Slowly, with a plan and willing to do whatever it takes
GEMINI	♊	With passion, energy and big ideas
CANCER	♋	Tentatively, with feeling and a great deal of care
LEO	♌	Wholeheartedly, passionately and creatively
VIRGO	♍	Gradually, with planning and attention to detail
LIBRA	♎	With style and consideration of every option
SCORPIO	♏	Quietly, with determination and passionate integrity
SAGITTARIUS	♐	Enthusiastically, with a well-thought out escape plan
CAPRICORN	♑	With control, determination and a keen eye on progress
AQUARIUS	♒	Alone, with conviction and no regard for the rules
PISCES	♓	Creatively, in sudden bursts, with faith in the universe

THE PLANETS:
THE SOCIAL PLANETS

Between the personal (see p10–13) and generational planets (see p18–21), lie the transpersonal or social planets Jupiter and Saturn. These reveal the lessons we're here to learn and how we might make our lives more expansive. They spend longer in each sign than the personal planets, presiding over lasting change as we grow, learn and develop. The house placements of the social and generational planets are as important as their sign placements so do check which astrological house (or area of life) these planets fall into in your birth chart. For more on the houses see p218-19.

JUPITER

THE LUCKY CHARM – RULER OF SAGITTARIUS & PISCES (CO-RULER)

The planet of luck and fortune reveals our innate talents and skills, showing us how we might harness these to make our lives feel full of potential. Jupiter is positive and outward looking, encouraging us to step out of our comfort zones and take the chances that make life more magical.

★ TIME SPENT IN EACH SIGN One year.

★ RETROGRADES Once a year.

★ COSMIC IMPACT Jupiter's movement through the signs brings positive energy and luck into our lives. You may feel this particularly when the planet takes a spin in your sun sign or when it returns to the position it was in at the time of your birth (this is your Jupiter Return, once every twelve years). On a collective level, we feel inspiration differently as Jupiter moves through the signs. Jupiter in Sagittarius feels optimistic and adventurous, encouraging us to follow our hearts and escape the status quo, while Jupiter in Capricorn drives us to make our own luck through our achievements.

YOUR JUPITER SIGN & WHERE YOUR TALENTS LIE

JUPITER IN		YOUR INNATE TALENTS
ARIES	♈	Leadership, trend spotting, big ideas, pushing boundaries to create change
TAURUS	♉	Investments, business, cooking, the natural world and anything involving aesthetics such as art, style and interiors
GEMINI	♊	Writing, speaking, self expression, ideas
CANCER	♋	Caring for others, making a difference, creating a wonderful home or family
LEO	♌	Being centre stage, entertaining people, networking your way to the top
VIRGO	♍	Problem solving, attention to detail, getting any job done
LIBRA	♎	Influencing others, keeping the peace, connecting people, style, beauty and fashion
SCORPIO	♏	Understanding power struggles, keeping secrets, careful research, attracting the support of others
SAGITTARIUS	♐	Making the most out of life, studying, sharing knowledge, moving between different cultures with ease
CAPRICORN	♑	Leadership, business, creating wealth, knowing what the next big thing will be
AQUARIUS	♒	Changing people's minds, gathering a crowd, standing up for the underdog
PISCES	♓	Creative pursuits, helping others heal, empathy, anything requiring imagination

SATURN

THE TEACHER – RULER OF CAPRICORN & AQUARIUS (CO-RULER)

The zodiac's karmic teacher Saturn is associated with life lessons, karma and growing up. Saturn likes to make sure we face up to our responsibilities and reveals what we are here to learn in life.

- ★ TIME SPENT IN EACH SIGN Two and a half years.
- ★ RETROGRADES Once a year.
- ★ COSMIC IMPACT As Saturn moves through the signs the lessons we learn in life change and evolve. With Saturn in Pisces themes of compassion, creativity and spirituality become front and centre in our lives, while Saturn in Aquarius urges us to gather together and create more equality in the world. Saturn's most recent change was March 2023, when it moved into Pisces. This means a new astrological house (and therefore area of your life; see p218–19 for more on the houses) becomes activated and impacted by its lessons. And when it returns to the position it was in when you were born – the infamous Saturn Return – it can really shake things up. This cosmic coming of age occurs every twenty-nine years, urging us to grow up, evolve and get real about where we're going in life.

YOUR SATURN SIGN & LIFE LESSONS

SATURN IN		THE LESSONS YOU'RE HERE TO LEARN
ARIES	♈	How to be yourself
TAURUS	♉	Self-worth and an abundant mindset
GEMINI	♊	How to speak up
CANCER	♋	How to be more vulnerable and create a sense of security
LEO	♌	How to step into the spotlight
VIRGO	♍	Work-life balance
LIBRA	♎	Being open to love (with boundaries!)
SCORPIO	♏	The power of transformation
SAGITTARIUS	♐	How to fit in anywhere and adapt
CAPRICORN	♑	How to win (without burning out)
AQUARIUS	♒	How to find your people and lead
PISCES	♓	How to put yourself first and quit the self-sabotage

To better understand your Saturn and Jupiter signs, look up the houses these planets fall into in your birth chart to discover what part of your life they are presiding over. See Dive Deeper on p218–19.

THE PLANETS:
THE GENERATIONAL PLANETS

The outer – or generational – planets are farther away from the sun and spend longer in each sign than the social or personal planets. This means they affect things in a more sweeping way than the faster-moving personal planets. You'll share your Uranus, Neptune and Pluto signs with many friends and connections of a similar age. These planets (and the houses they reside in our charts) offer insights into the ways we might rebel, the dreams that drive us and the transformations we might undergo in our lives.

URANUS

THE REBEL – CO-RULER OF AQUARIUS

Uranus is all about change, shake-ups and refusing to stay stuck in a box of society's making. Uranus doesn't really do comfort zones, bringing themes of invention, revolution and self-awareness to the table when we need it most.

★ TIME SPENT IN EACH SIGN Seven years.

★ RETROGRADES Once a year.

★ COSMIC IMPACT Uranus moves slowly through the signs (it takes eighty-four years to orbit the sun!), influencing the ways in which we personally and collectively innovate and create change in the world around us. While Uranus in Aries might usher in an era where individuality rules the roost, Uranus in Taurus puts themes of wealth and sustainability on the agenda for change.

YOUR URANUS SIGN & CHANGE

URANUS IN		HOW YOU'LL CREATE CHANGE
ARIES	♈	By being 100% yourself
TAURUS	♉	By caring about the environment
GEMINI	♊	By finding new ways to communicate
CANCER	♋	By creating an inclusive family
LEO	♌	By being creative
VIRGO	♍	By setting a good example
LIBRA	♎	By choosing to love
SCORPIO	♏	By refusing to conform
SAGITTARIUS	♐	By being willing to learn and adapt
CAPRICORN	♑	By making new rules
AQUARIUS	♒	By sticking it to The Man
PISCES	♓	By dreaming up a better world

NEPTUNE

THE MYSTIC – CO-RULER OF PISCES

If there's magic in the air, Neptune probably has a hand in it. This mystical planet is associated with our hopes and dreams, illusion and intuition. The position of Neptune in our charts can also reveal deep fears, challenges and ways in which we might become disillusioned.

- ★ TIME SPENT IN EACH SIGN Fourteen years.
- ★ RETROGRADES Once a year.
- ★ COSMIC IMPACT As Neptune moves through the signs it flavours our hopes and dreams with fresh energy. Neptune in Pisces is imaginative, creative and deeply spiritual, while Neptune in Aries brings a feisty and pioneering vibe to the collective conscious.

YOUR NEPTUNE SIGN & DREAMS

NEPTUNE IN		YOUR BIG DREAM
ARIES	♈	To be a trendsetter
TAURUS	♉	Financial freedom
GEMINI	♊	Becoming a thought leader
CANCER	♋	A truly happy family
LEO	♌	Fame
VIRGO	♍	Hitting every life goal on target
LIBRA	♎	Having it all
SCORPIO	♏	Being in charge
SAGITTARIUS	♐	Travel and freedom
CAPRICORN	♑	Wealth and success
AQUARIUS	♒	Freedom for all
PISCES	♓	Having magic powers

The astrological house these planets fall in is also very significant so check out Dive Deeper on p218-19.

PLUTO

THE TRANSFORMER – CO-RULER OF SCORPIO

A planet for astrological purposes (but officially downgraded to a dwarf planet in 2006), Pluto is associated with power, transformation, the underworld and destruction. The position of Pluto in our charts dictates the power struggles and personal evolutions we might undergo as we move through our lives.

- ★ TIME SPENT IN EACH SIGN Between twelve and thirty years.
- ★ RETROGRADES Once a year.
- ★ COSMIC IMPACT Pluto's shifts through the signs impacts society's systems of power and our collective approach to change and transformation. While Pluto is in Aquarius progress and equality rises to the top of the agenda but Pluto in Capricorn brings more of a traditional 'us and them' vibe.

YOUR PLUTO SIGN & POWER

PLUTO IN		WHERE YOU'LL FIND YOUR POWER
ARIES	♈	In style and self expression
TAURUS	♉	By creating wealth
GEMINI	♊	Through writing or speaking
CANCER	♋	By feeling at home somewhere
LEO	♌	In leadership
VIRGO	♍	By letting go of perfectionism
LIBRA	♎	In a marriage or partnership
SCORPIO	♏	By embracing your dark side
SAGITTARIUS	♐	Through learning and travel
CAPRICORN	♑	By playing the game
AQUARIUS	♒	By disrupting the status quo
PISCES	♓	By connecting with the cosmos

ASTROLOGICAL SEASONS OF 2024

Ready for a change of astrological weather? Check out the below for the dates the sun enters each sign in 2024. And don't panic if you're looking at this thinking, 'but I was born on 20 February and I'm an Aquarius!' You're almost certainly right! The date the sun enters each sign can vary by a day or two depending on your birth year. To double check what sign you are, check out your birth chart (see p6) or look up exactly what date the sun entered your sign the year you were born.

1 January–19 January	CAPRICORN SEASON CONTINUES
20 January–18 February	AQUARIUS SEASON
19 February–19 March	PISCES SEASON
20 March–18 April	ARIES SEASON
19 April–19 May	TAURUS SEASON
20 May–19 June	GEMINI SEASON
20 June–21 July	CANCER SEASON
22 July–21 August	LEO SEASON
22 August–21 September	VIRGO SEASON
22 September–21 October	LIBRA SEASON
22 October–20 November	SCORPIO SEASON
21 November–20 December	SAGITTARIUS SEASON
21 December–18 January 2025	CAPRICORN SEASON

WHEEL OF THE YEAR 2024

As the astrological seasons change, so too do the seasons of the year. The Wheel of the Year offers a framework of ancient festivities for magical seasonal celebration.

If you live in the southern hemisphere, your solstice and equinox celebrations will be at the opposite sides of this wheel.

A time to honour our ancestors while the veil is said to be at its thinnest.

The shortest day and longest night but a celebration of light to come as the days slowly stretch out towards spring.

An ancient fire festival celebrating the very first signs of spring.

A celebration of renewal, spring and the lighter, brighter days to come.

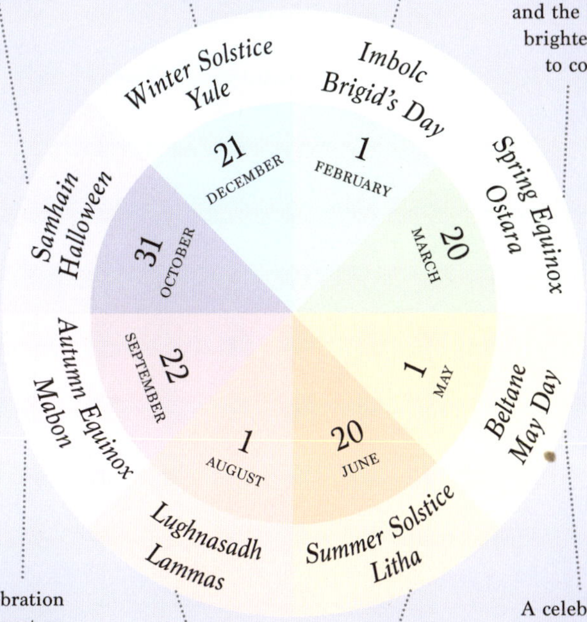

A celebration of harvest as day and night become equal once more.

A festival celebrating the beginning of the harvest.

The longest day and shortest night. Cue revelry, feasting and indulgence.

A celebration of the power of the sun and abundance to come.

MOONS OF 2024

11 January	*Thursday*	●	New moon	CAPRICORN
25 January	*Thursday*	○	Full moon	LEO
9 February	*Friday*	●	New moon (super moon)	AQUARIUS
24 February	*Saturday*	○	Full moon	VIRGO
10 March	*Sunday*	●	New moon (super moon)	PISCES
25 March	*Monday*	○	Full moon (lunar eclipse)	LIBRA
8 April	*Monday*	●	New moon (total solar eclipse)	ARIES
24 April	*Wednesday*	○	Full moon	SCORPIO
8 May	*Wednesday*	●	New moon	TAURUS
23 May	*Thursday*	○	Full moon	SAGITTARIUS
6 June	*Thursday*	●	New moon	GEMINI
22 June	*Saturday*	○	Full moon	CAPRICORN
5 July	*Friday*	●	New moon	CANCER
21 July	*Sunday*	○	Full moon	CAPRICORN
4 August	*Sunday*	●	New moon	LEO
19 August	*Monday*	○	Full moon (blue moon)	AQUARIUS
3 September	*Tuesday*	●	New moon	VIRGO
18 September	*Wednesday*	○	Full moon (super moon lunar eclipse)	PISCES
2 October	*Wednesday*	●	New moon (solar eclipse)	LIBRA
17 October	*Thursday*	○	Full moon (super moon)	ARIES
1 November	*Friday*	●	New moon	SCORPIO
15 November	*Friday*	○	Full moon	TAURUS
1 December	*Sunday*	●	New moon	SAGITTARIUS
15 December	*Sunday*	○	Full moon	GEMINI
30 December	*Monday*	●	New moon (black moon)	CAPRICORN

RETROGRADES OF 2024

Wondering why life feels crazy right now? There's probably a retrograde you can blame! See below for the dates of every retrograde in 2024.

Until 2 January	**Mercury Retrograde**	IN SAGITTARIUS
Until 27 January	**Uranus Retrograde**	IN TAURUS
1–25 April	**Mercury Retrograde**	IN ARIES
2 May–12 October	**Pluto Retrograde**	
	(2 May–2 September)	IN AQUARIUS
	(2 September–12 October)	IN CAPRICORN
29 June–15 November	**Saturn Retrograde**	IN PISCES
2 July–7 December	**Neptune Retrograde**	IN PISCES
5–28 August	**Mercury Retrograde**	
	(5–15 August)	IN VIRGO
	(15–28 August)	IN LEO
1 September–30 January 2025	**Uranus Retrograde**	IN TAURUS
9 October–4 February 2025	**Jupiter Retrograde**	IN GEMINI
26 November–15 December	**Mercury Retrograde**	IN SAGITTARIUS
6 December–24 February 2025	**Mars Retrograde**	
	(6 December–6 January 2025)	IN LEO

THE MODALITIES

For each sign in this book you'll see one of three modalities - cardinal, fixed and mutable - listed below. These are astrological qualities connected to groups of signs and knowing yours can help you understand the role you play in social dynamics and putting plans into action.

CARDINAL SIGNS
The Leaders

ARIES ♈
CANCER ♋
LIBRA ♎
CAPRICORN ♑

These signs start each season and are big on ideas, enthusiasm and determination. They might not always stick around to watch a mission play out but their original thinking and ability to gather support is the key to getting things going.

FIXED SIGNS
The Creators

TAURUS ♉
LEO ♌
SCORPIO ♏
AQUARIUS ♒

These signs fall in the middle of each season and have what it takes to get stuff done. They're the planners, the builders, the makers, the creators and the ones willing to follow through and put in the work that makes the magic happen.

MUTABLE SIGNS
The Perfectors

GEMINI ♊
VIRGO ♍
SAGITTARIUS ♐
PISCES ♓

These adaptable signs come at the end of each season, bringing go-with-the-flow energy. They're comfortable with change and can flex themselves to fit into any situation. Their seen-it-all-before vibe can be infuriating but they have what it takes to add the perfect finishing touch to any big idea.

THE ELEMENTS

Each sign is connected to an element and each element is said to represent certain qualities and areas of life. Understanding more about which sign is ruled by each can help us connect with and understand others (and ourselves) better.

FIRE	ARIES ♈ LEO ♌ SAGITTARIUS ♐	Passionate. Creative. Intense. Leaders with big ideas and the energy to make them happen.
EARTH	TAURUS ♉ VIRGO ♍ CAPRICORN ♑	Practical. Determined. Hard-working. Dependable, results-driven doers who love a plan, a goal and a win.
AIR	GEMINI ♊ LIBRA ♎ AQUARIUS ♒	Clever. Thoughtful. Expressive. Socially astute and creative thinkers who thrive on change and inspiration.
WATER	CANCER ♋ SCORPIO ♏ PISCES ♓	Imaginative. Intuitive. Emotional. Talented dreamers who feel things deeply and always find the magic in life.

JANUARY

CAPRICORN SEASON

♑

Welcome to Capricorn Season 30
Capricorn 31
Tune in to Capricorn Season 32
Starstruck: New Year's Day 33
Capricorn Season for Your Sign 34
Key Cosmic Dates 36
New Moon in Capricorn 38
Full Moon in Leo 40
Dive Deeper 2024:
Pluto in Aquarius 42
Pluto in Aquarius for Your Sign 44

WELCOME TO CAPRICORN SEASON

Farewell festive fun, hello January reset. A month filled with resolutions, good intentions and new gym leggings needs Capricorn at the cosmic helm. But not quite for the reason you think!

The clichés might be true – Capricorn really is driven, ambitious and determined to succeed – but no sea goat would ever sit around waiting for New Year to motivate them. Who needs resolutions when self-improvement is your year-round mission? Slowly, steadily, while the rest of us stare into space awaiting inspiration, Capricorn is out there making it happen. Building. Evolving. Planning. Climbing. Connecting. Taking the small steps that turn into big leaps, making real-life dreams come true. Capricorn is a sign forever reaching for the stars.

To know Capricorn is to love Capricorn – and if you're in a sea goat's inner circle you'll know it. Capricorn is loyal for life. Capricorn knows what's best for you. Capricorn will talk you off the edge. Capricorn is the mum of the friend group. The one who works out the bill. The pal who always rocks up with supplies – and spares of the supplies – and an umbrella just in case. This is the sign you want by your side should disaster ever strike.

That doesn't mean Capricorn is boring. There's a reason this sign is represented by the devil in tarot. Capricorn is a magician. A master of manifestation. Capricorn sees solutions where other people see problems and knows how to get what they want. They can see through fakes a mile off. Their expensive tastes keep them working hard but they're as happy cutting loose at a dive bar as they are sipping champagne.

Team up with Capricorn – in friendship, business or love – and it's power couple vibes all the way. If Capricorn has a plan and you're part of it, that plan is going to happen. This is a sign with razor-sharp instincts, plenty of commitment and a fierce need to win at life. January, February or any month of the year, Capricorn has got what it takes.

CAPRICORN

22 December 2023–19 January 2024

THE BOSS - *Ambitious. Hard-working. Reliable.*

SYMBOL	Sea goat
RULED BY	Saturn
ELEMENT	Earth
MODALITY	Cardinal
RULES THE	10th House of Career & Success
LUCKY DAY	Saturday
STAR STONE	Garnet
SOUL FLOWER	Carnation
AT THEIR BEST	High achieving, wise, practical
AT THEIR WORST	Ruthless, serious, overly sensible
TAROT CARD	The Devil

CAPRICORN 101

VIBE	Hard-working go-getter on a mission to succeed
STYLE	Elevated workwear, a capsule wardrobe, vintage labels
LOVES	Smashing a goal
HATES	Flaky timewasters
MOST LIKELY TO	Check emails on their day off
JUST DON'T	Mess with their schedule
FIND THEM	Working late, collecting an award, predicting the next big thing, bagging the corner office, ticking off life goals
BORN TO	Adult

TUNE IN TO CAPRICORN SEASON

Harness some sea goat spirit this January

WRITE A FIVE-YEAR PLAN There's nothing more Capricorn than a step-by-step plan. Ask yourself where you really want to be in five years and then break it down into achievable goals.

KNOW YOUR WORTH Money talks in Capricorn season so stop treating it like a dirty word. Is it time you asked for a pay rise? Turned a side hustle into a business? Demanded more from life?

PRIORITIZE YOUR GOALS Your goals. Not your partner's goals. Not your boss's goals. Your goals. Get clear on what you want to achieve this year and put those plans first on your agenda.

STREAMLINE YOUR LIFE Invest in 'Project You' with outsourcing, order and careful pre-planning. Think meal prep, hanging clothes in ready-to-go outfits or laminating a chores rota to stick on the fridge.

LOOK THE PART Dress for the job you want is pretty much Capricorn's life motto. Ditch the loungewear, elevate your outfit options and slip into something that says you mean business.

STARSTRUCK

NEW YEAR'S DAY

1 January

Whoever decided that the best way to ring in a New Year was with hangovers, health kicks and stress-inducing resolutions has a lot to answer for. The astrology of 1 January 2024 invites us to consider a more gentle approach to turning the page. Yes, we have a brand new 366 days (it's a leap year!) to make our own but no it doesn't have to start with a bang right this second. Read on for ways to ease into the New Year vibe.

CREATE A VISION BOARD

Try a more creative way to express your hopes and dreams for the year to come. Light a candle, play some relaxing music and take your time over making an inspiring collage of photos and images that speak to your soul.

GO ON A WONDER WALK

Turn the traditional New Year's Day stroll into something more healing with an unplanned roam around your neighbourhood. Wrap up warm, breathe deeply, take a few wrong turns, go where the mood takes you, allow your mind to wander and look for signs, both literal and nature-based, that you're on the right path.

WAIT IT OUT

The year begins with the moon waning in Virgo and messenger planet Mercury retrograde (see p90–3 for more) so if you're not really feeling it, you can totally blame the cosmos. Take your time thinking, dreaming and planning and you might find 2 January (when Mercury resumes direct motion) or even 11 January (the first new moon of 2024) have more New Year energy for you.

CAPRICORN SEASON FOR YOUR SIGN

♈ ARIES New Year, new Aries? It's time for you to dream bigger than ever when it comes to your career as Capricorn season kicks off with a planetary pile-up in your success zone. Think promotions, new projects and finally getting that business idea up and running.

If you do one thing this month: Finish what you started.

♉ TAURUS Let 'think big' be your January motto as Capricorn season hones in on your adventurous 9th House. Big travel plans (possibly involving work) or mind-expanding study look lit for Taurus as 2024 begins.

If you do one thing this month: Check the date on your passport.

♊ GEMINI Trust your instincts this Capricorn season because energy doesn't lie. Making a big commitment to something (or someone) could pay off for you this month but make sure you're doing it for the right reasons.

If you do one thing this month: Let your intuition be your guide.

♋ CANCER Dynamic duos of all kinds are in focus for you right now. And if you don't ask, you don't get! If you're ready to take a relationship (business or pleasure) to the next level now is the perfect time to make a move.

If you do one thing this month: Tell someone how you feel.

♌ LEO Dust off your trainers and down that green juice, it's New Year clichés all the way for Leo. A health kick that fell by the wayside in 2023 is ready for a reboot.

If you do one thing this month: Put yourself first.

♍ VIRGO Ready for your close up? You better be. Good times, creative success and a spell in the spotlight are all on the cards for Virgo as January hits its stride.

If you do one thing this month: Put yourself out there.

♎ LIBRA Make plans related to your home, family or living situation as January begins and the path ahead could soon become clearer. Creating a strong foundation upon which to build your life is a power move for you right now.

If you do one thing this month: Make the move.

♏ SCORPIO You usually play your cards close to your chest but there's something you're itching to say or share this Capricorn season. Tell it like it is, speak your truth and know that the world is finally ready to hear what you have to say.

If you do one thing this month: Trust the process.

♐ SAGITTARIUS Money talks for Sagittarius as 2024 begins and that means finally getting to grips with your financial situation. Make finding ways to boost your bank balance a priority and you'll soon be cashing in.

If you do one thing this month: Ask for more.

♑ CAPRICORN It's birthday season, it's New Year and between the new moon and a pile up of planets in your sign, it's all going on for Capricorn in 2024. Ready for a reset? You better be.

If you do one thing this month: Prioritize a big dream.

♒ AQUARIUS It's time to put your mental health and wellbeing first as you ease in to the New Year. A spiritual practice that makes you feel inspired could be the key that unlocks the next magical phase of your life.

If you do one thing this month: Meditate.

♓ PISCES Connections count for Pisces this Capricorn season so get out there and make some. A meeting of minds that offers a much-needed career boost is not to be missed.

If you do one thing this month: Make the call.

JANUARY

Key Cosmic Dates

MERCURY RETROGRADE ENDS *2 January*	Time to stop blaming everything on our favourite cosmic scapegoat. Expect stalled travel plans to start to come together.
MARS ENTERS CAPRICORN *4 January*	Ready for some next-level go-getter energy? Mars in Capricorn invites you to take charge of your destiny and pursue goals with determination.
NEW MOON IN CAPRICORN *11 January*	If your year hasn't got off on the right foot, consider this new moon your reset button. Take a deep breath, shake off any residual 2023 angst and make plans for the year ahead.
MERCURY ENTERS CAPRICORN *14 January*	Ready to create some method in the madness? Mercury in Capricorn is all about methodical step-by-step approaches that get stuff done.
AQUARIUS SEASON BEGINS *20 January*	Forward-thinking, freedom-seeking, independent Aquarius takes the cosmic reigns today.
PLUTO ENTERS AQUARIUS *21 January*	Change, progress, power to the people... Pluto's shift into Aquarius is the month's biggest astro news (see p42–5).
VENUS ENTERS CAPRICORN *23 January*	Time to put a ring on it? Venus in Capricorn invites us to level up, commit and take love more seriously.

FULL MOON IN LEO
25 January

Let go of anything that's been stealing your joy as we move into the final week of January.

URANUS RETROGRADE ENDS
27 January

The life shake-up you've been waiting for is here. Uranus direct in Taurus urges us to find the magic that lies just outside our comfort zones.

RETROGRADE (RX) PLANETS

MERCURY RX
until 2 January
(in Sagittarius)

URANUS RX
until 27 January
(in Taurus)

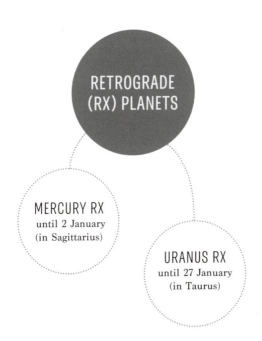

Thursday
11
January
2024

NEW MOON IN CAPRICORN

London 11:57 | New York 06:57 | Los Angeles 03:57 | Tokyo 20:57 | Sydney 22:57

A new moon in earthy, practical Capricorn offers up an extra hit of reset energy when we need it most. This is the best time in the lunar cycle to set intentions, a bit like a mini monthly New Year, so spend some time getting real with yourself about where you're headed and how you're going to get there. It's time to make a plan, Capricorn-style!

Moon times can differ by a second depending on the rounding method used to calculate them. So don't worry if you see a slightly different time elsewhere! The vibes still apply.

NEW MOON INTENTIONS FOR YOUR SIGN

Power up your plans as a new moon cycle begins

ARIES	♈	Take the first step towards making a 'big picture' dream happen.
TAURUS	♉	Set a goal that involves learning or education and your life could change forever.
GEMINI	♊	Recommit to a passion project for a next-level payoff.
CANCER	♋	Use the power of the new moon to call in your dream relationship.
LEO	♌	Switch up your daily routine to create magical change in your life.
VIRGO	♍	Set intentions that put joy, fun and creativity first and you'll soar.
LIBRA	♎	Conjure up your dream home with a new moon wish.
SCORPIO	♏	The truth matters this new moon so set your bravest and most honest intention yet.
SAGITTARIUS	♐	Financial goals and intentions made this new moon are set to come good.
CAPRICORN	♑	Consider this your personal New Year and set an intention to match.
AQUARIUS	♒	Set an intention that makes your mental health and wellbeing a non-negotiable priority.
PISCES	♓	Invite a magical meeting of minds into your life this new moon.

Friday
25
January
2024

FULL MOON IN LEO

London 17:54 | New York 12:54 | Los Angeles 09:54 | Tokyo 02:54 26 January | Sydney 04:54 26 January

The first full moon of the year is always a big moment and this month's Wolf Moon in Leo is no exception. Leo full moons invite us to seek more joy and put fun back on the agenda – just what we need as January plays out. There's always plenty of magic in the air on the full moon, making it a great time for manifesting goals and wishing for a dream to come true. It's also the start of the moon's waning phase, which makes it a great time to let go of anything that's holding you back.

FULL MOON THEMES & QUESTIONS FOR YOUR SIGN

	THEMES	ASK YOURSELF
ARIES ♈	Fun, flirtation and creative success	*Am I ready to take a chance on a big dream?*
TAURUS ♉	Dreaming, planning and working out what home and family mean to you	*Is it time I moved on from the drama?*
GEMINI ♊	Writing, speaking, connecting and creating	*Am I brave enough to tell someone how I really feel?*
CANCER ♋	Knowing your worth and asking for more	*Why am I still playing small?*
LEO ♌	Big life realizations	*Who do I want to become?*
VIRGO ♍	Resting, thinking and taking time out	*What do I need closure on?*

Attune to the magic of the Leo full moon

	THEMES	ASK YOURSELF
LIBRA ♎	Re-evaluating your friendships and social circle	*Who am I with when I feel my best?*
SCORPIO ♏	Reaching for the stars in your career	*Is it time I stopped sabotaging my own goals?*
SAGITTARIUS ♐	Travel, learning and expanding your mind	*What would I do if life had no limits?*
CAPRICORN ♑	Facing up to your own role in a tricky relationship dynamic	*What would happen if I stopped being so self-critical?*
AQUARIUS ♒	Teaming up in life, love or business	*Could sacrificing freedom now pay off later down the line?*
PISCES ♓	Big realizations about your life, health and routine	*What needs to go for me to start living my best life?*

DIVE DEEPER 2024:
PLUTO IN AQUARIUS

21 January

Are you ready for an energy shift that changes the fabric of both your life and the lives of those around you? Buckle up! Planet of transformation Pluto moves from serious, traditional Capricorn into forward-thinking, humanitarian Aquarius on 21 January, bringing some serious regeneration vibes our way.

We had a mini preview in spring 2023 when the planet took a spin through Aquarius from late March to mid June. But this time, bar a retrograde back into Capricorn later this year, the planet known as the great revealer is here to stay a while (until 2043 to be precise!).

Like Neptune and Uranus, Pluto is what's known as an outer or generational planet in astrology. These planets move very slowly through the signs (Pluto spends up to thirty years in one sign) meaning their impact is felt on more of a collective level. That doesn't mean you won't feel the impact of this cosmic shift personally though. You just won't feel it alone. We're all in it together with Pluto in Aquarius. And change can be a good thing, especially with the water-bearer air sign at the helm.

POWER TO THE PEOPLE

Aquarius is the zodiac's community-minded humanitarian. It's a sign that values freedom, believes in a better future for everyone and isn't afraid to take a stand. Aquarius is modern, rebellious, forward-thinking, space-age even – a tech-savvy sign that's always ready to shake things up. Add the transformative powers of Pluto and we might just have an uprising on our hands, one that changes the world for the greater good of everyone...

Collectively and personally Pluto in Aquarius is a long-game affair. Nothing changes if nothing changes but nothing changes overnight either. Think slow-dawning realizations, step-by-step changes that make a difference and ripping up the rule book to start again. Power to the people... and power to you as you change, evolve and step into your future.

THEMES OF PLUTO IN AQUARIUS

- Community spirit, communal living, sustainability
- Shifts in society, possible corruption, playing fields being levelled
- Technology upgrades, digital everything, space-age innovation
- Cosmic downloads, spirituality, new-age thinking
- Secrets, taboos, making peace with our dark sides
- Rebellion, freedom-seeking, sticking it to The Man
- Equality, equity, sharing resources

PLUTO IN AQUARIUS FOR YOUR SIGN

Pluto's impact is more collective than personal but there are still themes this transit may begin to bring to light for you.

♈ ARIES Notice who you feel your best with, because your social circle is transforming. Is it time you levelled up? Made peace with a friendship lost? Began finding your people? Remember you're a leader not a follower, Aries.

Transformation: You were born to lead and your people are gathering.

♉ TAURUS Pluto in Aquarius spells big change ahead for you and your career but we're talking long game. Small steps you take now could lead to you finding success when you expect it least. You have the power.

Transformation: Trust your instincts at work to leave a legacy.

♊ GEMINI It's all about the bigger picture for you, Gemini. Exploring something that fascinates you could become the start of an exciting travel, education or spiritual adventure.

Transformation: Think beyond the world, religion or life you were born into.

♋ CANCER For you, Pluto in Aquarius could spell the start of sharing time, energy and resources with someone significant. Perhaps a marriage, commitment or business venture is on the cards? Whichever, whatever, it's life-changing stuff.

Transformation: A wise investment could become what you need to reinvent yourself.

♌ LEO An unconventional but life-altering relationship, friendship or passion project could eventually change everything for you.

Transformation: Put yourself out there and let your lion heart guide you.

♍ VIRGO Changes to your health, wellbeing and daily routine made now could change the trajectory of your life. Think bad habits ditched long term and work-life balance nailed.

Transformation: You know what you need to do to make your life healthier and happier. Start now.

♎ LIBRA Seek pleasure in everything you do and the rest will follow, Libra. Pluto invites you to choose a life of good times, magic and creative wonder. Are you brave enough?

Transformation: Remember what lit you up when you were younger? Can you find your way back?

♏ SCORPIO Creating a strong foundation upon which to build your future is key for you now. Think renting or buying a home, starting (or adding to!) a family and slowly separating yourself from the life you were born into so you can make a future on your own terms.

Transformation: Working out what family and home mean to you (traditional or otherwise) paves a magical path.

♐ SAGITTARIUS Pluto in Aquarius could see you sharing your voice, story or cause with the world. This might not be entirely comfortable for you but a project related to writing, speaking or sharing something deeply personal could play an important role in your future.

Transformation: Slowly but surely you're finding the words to change your life.

♑ CAPRICORN Money talks in Capricorn world and Pluto in Aquarius is all in for the payoff. Think next-level changes of circumstances, big-time investment and taking a considered risk or gamble on something you know will yield results.

Transformation: This is where you create the future you know you deserve.

♒ AQUARIUS Pluto's spin in your sign ushers in a period of intense personal growth and development. Ready to rise? You better be.

Transformation: You're changing and evolving from the inside out. Trust your intuition and go with the flow.

♓ PISCES It's time to heal, rest, evolve and seek closure on anything and everything that's been holding you back. Pluto in Aquarius invites you to let it all go so you can rebuild stronger and better than ever.

Transformation: Your inner world holds the keys to your outer world. A spiritual practice might just change your life.

FEBRUARY

AQUARIUS SEASON

♒

Welcome to Aquarius Season **48**
Aquarius **49**
Tune in to Aquarius Season **50**
Starstruck: Valentine's Day **51**
Aquarius Season for Your Sign **52**
Key Cosmic Dates **54**
New Moon in Aquarius **56**
Full Moon in Virgo **58**

WELCOME TO AQUARIUS SEASON

Hibernation mode is officially cancelled! Allow Aquarius season to dislodge you from the sofa and fling you back into the real world this February. The long dark nights aren't over yet but air sign Aquarius (yes, this is an air sign, despite the watery connotations) has no time for fading loungewear or New Year deprivation regimes. It's time to ditch the detox, ghost Netflix and get your 2024 game face on.

The zodiac's eco-conscious free-thinker is always one step ahead, forever ready to stand up for the underdog and stick it to The Man. They love people, parties and spontaneous meetings of minds. They excel at bright ideas and bringing people together. They love a crowd but they'll never follow one. Aquarius is a true original, a sign that knows how to change minds and rage against the machine in a way that actually makes a difference. For the water bearer, rules are always made to be broken.

For this sign friendship, freedom and equality are everything. Aquarius wants to be free to be who they want to be and do what they want to do but they also want everyone else to have the same opportunity. Their tendency to flit between friendship groups and eschew commitment can make them seem emotionally cold at times, but allow them the space to be themselves and their loyalty knows no bounds.

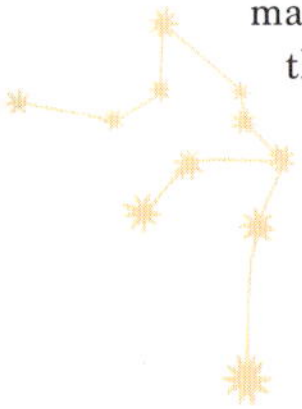

Quirky, offbeat and a little out there, team up with Aquarius and you'll never be bored again. Allow the water bearer to take the reins and you'll be plotting social reform one minute and dancing to space-age beats at a warehouse rave the next. Forget reaching for the stars, Aquarius has launched a rocket and is already flying among them.

AQUARIUS

20 January–18 February

THE FREE SPIRIT - *Independent. Forward-thinking. Original.*

SYMBOL	Water bearer
RULED BY	Uranus and Saturn (co-ruler)
ELEMENT	Air
MODALITY	Fixed
RULES THE	11th House of Friendship & Community
LUCKY DAY	Saturday
STAR STONE	Amethyst
SOUL FLOWER	Orchid
AT THEIR BEST	Free-spirited, idealistic, humanitarian
AT THEIR WORST	Judgemental, aloof, controlling
TAROT CARD	The Star

AQUARIUS 101

VIBE	Outspoken rebel with a cause
STYLE	Effortlessly cool, accidental trendsetter, niche labels, customization, crystals with everything
LOVES	A party
HATES	Feeling tied down
MOST LIKELY TO	Change the world
JUST DON'T	Ask them to stay home on a Saturday night
FIND THEM	Running between social events, on a justice march, disrupting their industry, on a plant medicine retreat, gazing at the stars
BORN TO	Fight the system

TUNE IN TO AQUARIUS SEASON

Channel some water-bearer vibes

PAY IT FORWARD There's nothing more Aquarian than fighting for a cause. Start a campaign, fundraise, join a local action group and get passionate.

BE WEIRD Aquarius is different in the best possible way and so, of course, are you. Step out of the shadows, own your offbeat side and don't be afraid to be yourself.

FIND YOUR PEOPLE Power to the people is Aquarius's rallying cry! Gather your mates for a celebration, join a club, create a community and find power in numbers.

GO SOLO Freedom is the lifeblood of Aquarius. Embrace the independent spirit of this sign with a solo trip somewhere special. Dare to date yourself!

TAKE A LEAP Tradition dictates that the 29 February is a date where women can propose to men but not even folklore could persuade Aquarius to follow such a rule. Instead use this bonus day to make a bold move that's all your own and step out of your comfort zone.

GET EXPERIMENTAL Aquarius is a true visionary, forever one step ahead. Tap into the thrill of the new by investing in cutting-edge tech or seeking inspiration from up-and-coming writers, artists and musicians.

MAKE A VISION HAPPEN Aquarian energy is all about bold moves and breakout ideas. Got a business idea or creative vision you want to make reality? Be a disrupter, challenge authority and stop at nothing as you make it happen.

SAVE THE PLANET Channel some Aquarian eco-vibes by ditching plastic, going vegan and actually remembering to take a reusable bag to the shops.

STARSTRUCK

VALENTINE'S DAY

14 February

Love it or hate it, the most clichéd day in the romance calendar is an Aquarius season main event. Not that Aquarius would ever settle for an identikit bouquet and table-for-two sitch. Go your own way this V-Day by putting self-love at the top of the agenda whether you're loved up, looking or have sworn off romance for life.

COSMIC SELF-LOVE FOR YOUR SIGN

FIRE SIGNS	*Aries* *Leo* *Sagittarius*	Take yourself out. Shower yourself in gifts. Book an escape with your BFF. Big up that main character energy. Take your best-ever selfie. Share it widely.
EARTH SIGNS	*Taurus* *Virgo* *Capricorn*	Take a duvet day. Spend time in nature. Practise yoga. Read a self-help book. Light a fancy candle. Have a massage. Invest in silk sheets. Go to bed. Stay there.
AIR SIGNS	*Gemini* *Libra* *Aquarius*	Listen to an inspiring podcast. Get creative. Meditate. Talk to a friend. Create a beautiful tablescape. Try a soundbath. Buy a crystal. Aura spray the world.
WATER SIGNS	*Cancer* *Scorpio* *Pisces*	Make a nostalgic playlist. Feel some feelings. Head to the sea. Swim. Get dressed up. Dance like crazy. Burn incense. Pretend you're a mermaid. Cast a spell.

AQUARIUS SEASON FOR YOUR SIGN

♈ **ARIES** Expect locked eyes across a crowded room to change your world this month, Aries. A new connection offering the leg-up you need in life, love or business is waiting for you to notice them.

If you do one thing this month: Accept the invitation.

♉ **TAURUS** A next-level career goal you set a long time ago could begin to come good this month. You really didn't come this far to only come this far, Taurus!

If you do one thing this month: Keep your work-life balance in check.

♊ **GEMINI** It's time to broaden your horizons, Gemini. What truly fascinates you? Where have you always wanted to go? Follow your heart on this one.

If you do one thing this month: Say YES to a big adventure.

♋ **CANCER** An all-consuming love affair could see you blowing caution to the wind this month. Expect fireworks by Valentine's Day. Just try not to lose too much of yourself in the process.

If you do one thing this month: Think twice.

♌ **LEO** Ready to level up in life or love, Leo? This month could see you asking (or answering) a very big question about your future. Are you ready to become part of a power couple?

If you do one thing this month: Commit.

♍ **VIRGO** This is the month to get yourself out a rut, make a big change and stick with it, Virgo. A shake-up to your life, health or daily routine is long overdue.

If you do one thing this month: Prioritize your wellbeing.

♎ **LIBRA** If you've been waiting for the right time to get back out on the dating scene, start a creative project or simply enjoy life more, the time is now. Your star is rising, Libra.

If you do one thing this month: Believe in yourself.

♏ **SCORPIO** 'Home is where the heart is' rings true for you this month. It's time to embrace your chosen family and live life on your own terms.

If you do one thing this month: Do it your way.

♐ **SAGITTARIUS** An exciting project related to writing, speaking or sharing your story could change your world.

If you do one thing this month: Speak your truth.

♑ **CAPRICORN** Be ready to pounce on a new job offer, promotion or dream investment opportunity, Capricorn. Money talks and your luck is in.

If you do one thing this month: Say YES.

♒ **AQUARIUS** The fresh start you've been waiting for is finally here. Believe in yourself, push forwards and don't look back.

If you do one thing this month: Take action.

♓ **PISCES** It's time to let go of something that's been holding you back for far too long, Pisces. Stop getting in your own way.

If you do one thing this month: Seek closure.

FEBRUARY

Key Cosmic Dates

IMBOLC
1 February

An ancient celebration of the start of the sowing season, Saint Brigid and the very first signs of the spring to come.

MERCURY ENTERS AQUARIUS
5 February

Get set for some big conversations, breakthrough ideas and possible information overload.

NEW MOON IN AQUARIUS
9 February

This super new moon is perfect for creating plans, contributing to your community or calling in a dream collaboration.

LUNAR NEW YEAR
10 February

The lunar new year is celebrated by many across the globe - 2024 ushers in the Year of the Dragon.

MARS ENTERS AQUARIUS
13 February

Want to make the world a better place? Mars in Aquarius brings big humanitarian energy to the cosmic table.

VENUS ENTERS AQUARIUS
16 February

A reminder that love doesn't have to look like it does in the movies. Romance on your own terms starts here.

PISCES SEASON BEGINS
19 February

Get creative, feel all the feelings, sleep, dream, dance, cry... it's Pisces season.

MERCURY ENTERS PISCES
23 February

Pay attention to the messages in your dreams as Mercury takes a spin in Pisces.

FULL MOON IN VIRGO
24 February

Time to quit the self-sabotage, create space in your life and start believing you have what it takes.

LEAP YEAR
29 February

An extra day of magic to do with what you will.

NO RETROGRADES

FRIDAY
9
February
2024

NEW MOON IN AQUARIUS

London 22:59 | New York 17:59 | Los Angeles 14:59 | Tokyo 07:59 10 February | Sydney 09:59 10 February

A super new moon in progressive Aquarius ushers in a positivity power-up and then some. This is the ideal new moon for changemakers, activists and anyone on a mission to find their people and to set intentions that create action. Want to change the world? You've got this! Ready to go your own way? That too! Dreaming about setting up a space-age commune in some distant, magical land? Not as far out as you think. The future is yours with an Aquarius new moon!

NEW MOON INTENTIONS FOR YOUR SIGN

It's fresh-start vibes all round

ARIES	♈	Invest in a new friendship group, community or social scene that makes you feel alive.
TAURUS	♉	Commit to prioritizing a side hustle or passion project.
GEMINI	♊	Sign up to a course of study or start planning a big trip somewhere inspiring.
CANCER	♋	Be honest about what really brings you pleasure in life and follow that path.
LEO	♌	Make the first move in life, love or business deals this new moon.
VIRGO	♍	Set a goal that prioritizes your health and make sure you stick with it.
LIBRA	♎	Make time to rediscover a childhood passion.
SCORPIO	♏	Start planning for a new addition to your home or family life.
SAGITTARIUS	♐	Dare to share your big idea, plan or story with the world.
CAPRICORN	♑	Think big (and then bigger) when it comes to your financial future.
AQUARIUS	♒	Leave no area of your life unturned as you set wheels in motion for a major personal overhaul.
PISCES	♓	Set an intention that puts spiritual practice at the centre of your world.

Super moons are closer to Earth and so appear larger and brighter than usual when they occur on a full moon. You can't see a super new moon but you might find you feel its cosmic impact more.

Saturday
24
February
2024

FULL MOON IN VIRGO

London 12:30 | New York 07:30 | Los Angeles 04:30 | Tokyo 21:30 | Sydney 23:30

February's magical Snow Moon falls in diligent and discerning Virgo, shining a light on the daily routines and habits that make our lives run smoothly (or not so smoothly). This is the perfect full moon to let go of old habits no longer serving you and bring renewed vigour to a health kick or work project. It's also a good time to release yourself of self-criticism and know you are already enough.

FULL MOON THEMES & QUESTIONS FOR YOUR SIGN

	THEMES	ASK YOURSELF
ARIES ♈	Health, wellbeing and daily routines	*How can I get my life and health back on track again?*
TAURUS ♉	Fun, flirtation and good vibes galore	*How can I find more time for the things that light me up?*
GEMINI ♊	Family responsibilities, domestic issues, home renovations	*Can I take something off my plate right now?*
CANCER ♋	Speaking your truth even if it feels impossible at times	*What do I need to get out in the open to move forwards?*
LEO ♌	Investing in yourself, knowing your worth, thinking big	*What do I need to take my life to the next level?*
VIRGO ♍	Starting over, self-belief, a new look or project	*What limiting beliefs am I leaving behind this full moon?*

Attune to the magic of the Virgo full moon

	THEMES	ASK YOURSELF
LIBRA ♎	Looking within, getting spiritual, realizing there's more to life	*What can I stop doing to make more time for myself?*
SCORPIO ♏	Community spirit, parties, invitations and social events	*How can I step out of my comfort zone?*
SAGITTARIUS ♐	Work, success and focusing on your future self	*What is stopping me from aiming higher?*
CAPRICORN ♑	Travel plans, big dreams, mind-expanding journeys	*What is stopping me from making a dream reality?*
AQUARIUS ♒	Personal transformation, shared resources and money, secrets and lies	*Who do I need to keep on side?*
PISCES ♓	Big change ahead for a romance that matters	*Could redressing the give-and-take balance improve a relationship?*

MARCH

PISCES SEASON

♓

Welcome to Pisces Season 62
Pisces 63
Tune in to Pisces Season 64
Starstruck: Spring Equinox 65
Pisces Season for Your Sign 66
Key Cosmic Dates 68
New Moon in Pisces 70
Full Moon Eclipse in Libra 72
Dive Deeper 2024:
Eclipse Season 74
The Eclipses of 2024 76

WELCOME TO PISCES SEASON

Think of Pisces season as a spring clean for the soul. There's a time and a place for leaping into frantic action but now is not it. Pisces is a sign that understands the magic of the in-between, so allow yourself to drift with the tide and embrace a season of dreaming, healing and knowing that every ending is a beginning in disguise.

Sign of psychics, creatives and visionaries, Pisces is the zodiac's mystical mermaid, happiest barefoot, fancy-free and – ideally – by the water. Pisces might not be able to make a decision to save their life or ever show up on time for your birthday dinner, but their ability to make life feel like one long daydream is irresistible. They know what you're thinking before you know what you're thinking. Pisces can make you fall in love with them in the blink of an eye, and couldn't care less about wealth or status. Pisces has the creative power to turn heartbreak into inspiration, dead ends into fresh starts and a definite 'No' into 'Okay, maybe' in no time at all.

This water sign is also a master of endings. Grief? Heartbreak? General ennui? Feeling feelings is a full-time job for these intuitive and emotional souls. If you want to wallow, they'll wallow beside you. If you want to down cocktails until you can't remember your own name, they'll happily do that too. And the moment you're ready to start talking revenge looks or one-way tickets to Bali, they'll be right by your side brandishing passports and credit cards.

If you think you know Pisces you probably need to think again but having one on your side is always a power move. Loyal, generous and endlessly creative, Pisces wants everyone they love to live the dream. And with their otherworldly manifestation skills they might just make it happen.

PISCES

19 February–19 March

THE DREAMER - *Creative. Flaky. Sensitive. Psychic.*

SYMBOL	Fish
RULED BY	Neptune and Jupiter (co-ruler)
ELEMENT	Water
MODALITY	Mutable
RULES THE	12th House of Endings, Spirituality & the Subconscious
LUCKY DAY	Thursday
STAR STONE	Aquamarine
SOUL FLOWER	Water lily
AT THEIR BEST	Creative, spiritual, intuitive, flexible
AT THEIR WORST	Disorganized, distracted, indecisive, overly sensitive
TAROT CARD	The Moon

PISCES 101

VIBE	Mystical mermaid living in a fantasy world
STYLE	Barefoot, beach-bound bohemian, long hair, sequins, floaty layers
LOVES	A king-size bed
HATES	Feeling under pressure
MOST LIKELY TO	Create a masterpiece
JUST DON'T	Bother them with any practical stuff
FIND THEM	Gazing into the middle distance, pressing snooze on their alarm clock, swimming in the sea, waiting for a miracle, fantasizing, crying prettily
BORN TO	Daydream

TUNE IN TO PISCES SEASON

Allow yourself to float in on the tide

TRUST THE UNIVERSE Pisces knows that what's meant for them won't pass them by. Embrace the flow of life this month without trying to control the outcome. If it comes, let it, if it goes, let it.

MANIFEST If any sign has a direct line to the universe it's Pisces. Up your manifestation game with a moon ritual or write a wish list to the cosmos and know that magic awaits.

SLEEP Pisces is a sign that loves to sleep. Big up your bedtime with new sheets, soothing scents and sounds or a swanky silk eye-mask.

PAY ATTENTION TO YOUR DREAMS Dreaming big is a way of life for these magical fish. Put a notebook and pen by your bed to scribble down the dreams and ideas that hit when your mind relaxes.

GET SPIRITUAL Pisces season is the ideal time to start a meditation or yoga practice, try tarot or oracle cards and explore the workings of your mind. Let your intuition lead the way.

CREATE, CREATE, CREATE Write, paint, cook, sew, design, plant, craft or make something - anything, as long as it taps into your creative side.

TAKE THE PRESSURE OFF Make the most of this month's dreamy, laid-back vibe by cutting yourself some slack for a change. More breaks! More downtime! More staring into space!

IMMERSE YOURSELF It wouldn't be Pisces season if you didn't take the time to sink into a hot bath or dive into the sea. Even if an outdoor dip feels out of the question right now, simply being close to water is a great way to harness the energy of Pisces.

STARSTRUCK

SPRING EQUINOX

20 March

A powerful celebration of rebirth and renewal, spring equinox - autumn equinox in the southern hemisphere - marks the moment the sun passes the celestial equator, allowing night and day to fall into balance. It also signals the beginning of the astrological New Year as the sun enters fiery go-getting Aries. All this makes it the perfect time to inject some energy into your daily routine, step outside your comfort zone and celebrate the magic of life!

COSMIC WAYS TO MARK THE SPRING EQUINOX

THROW A PARTY

Step into spring with a magical equinox party. Invite friends to bring a favourite dish. Create some delicious cocktails. Make flower crowns. Paint eggs. Set intentions for the new season by a crackling outdoor fire. Light candles and make wishes. Celebrate new beginnings.

GO FORAGING

Now is the ideal time to forage for wild garlic and elderflowers in the great outdoors. Allow your mind to wander towards hopes, dreams and plans for the future as you lose yourself in nature.

SPRING CLEAN

Celebrate new beginnings and renewal with a massive clear out. Donate old clothes and household items to create space for the magic to come in your life, then spring clean everything you can get your hands on. Scent your space with energizing essential oils (try lemon or peppermint).

PLANT A GARDEN

Plant flower, vegetable or herb seeds in a window box, small pot or garden and make wishes for the future as you water them. Watch and wait. Nurture them. Celebrate their growth.

HAVE A MAKEOVER

Ready to shake off the shackles of a life that's feeling too small for where you're headed? You may as well look the part! Invest in yourself with some healthy living, bold style statements and a brave new season attitude.

PISCES SEASON FOR YOUR SIGN

♈ ARIES Taking time out doesn't come easy for you but this month has downtime written all over it. Embrace stillness and you just might hit upon your best idea yet.

If you do one thing this month: Take it slow.

♉ TAURUS A change in circumstances could see a whole new community of people come into your life this month. Expect magic in a meeting of minds.

If you do one thing this month: Leave the past behind.

♊ GEMINI This is the big one for your career, Gemini. Your hard work is about to pay off in the best possible way.

If you do one thing this month: Shine brighter than ever.

♋ CANCER Plans for the trip of a lifetime could begin to take shape this month. Where have you always wanted to go? And who with?

If you do one thing this month: Book the trip.

♌ LEO A new obsession could spell the end of something this Pisces season. Go with the flow. Your heart knows what it wants.

If you do one thing this month: Accept change.

♍ VIRGO A power partnership with life-changing potential could come into your life this month. Think business deals, friends in high places or signing on an exciting dotted line.

If you do one thing this month: Allow your star to rise.

♎ **LIBRA** It's time to get back on track with a health goal that's fallen by the wayside. You're not too old and it's not too late.

If you do one thing this month: Put yourself first.

♏ **SCORPIO** A childhood passion or dream could inspire you in more ways than one this month. It's time to truly embrace your quirks, Scorpio.

If you do one thing this month: Look back for inspiration.

♐ **SAGITTARIUS** A big move or renovation project could take up a lot of headspace for you this month. Try not to run before you can walk on this one.

If you do one thing this month: Create a haven.

♑ **CAPRICORN** The words you speak matter more than ever now, Capricorn. Use your powers of persuasion wisely and you'll soon get what you want.

If you do one thing this month: Ask the big question.

♒ **AQUARIUS** It's time to bite the bullet with a big investment in yourself and your plans for the future. Speculate to accumulate!

If you do one thing this month: Dive on in.

♓ **PISCES** It's your favourite time of year to make plans, dream big and manifest some magic. Make it happen, Pisces!

If you do one thing this month: Hit the refresh button.

MARCH

Key Cosmic Dates

NEW MOON IN PISCES
10 March

Time to set some fresh intentions that leave the past behind this super new moon.

MERCURY ENTERS ARIES
10 March

The act now, think later, go-getting energy boost we've been waiting for.

VENUS ENTERS PISCES
11 March

Living the dream starts to feel possible with the love planet in mystical Pisces.

ARIES SEASON BEGINS/ ASTROLOGICAL NEW YEAR
20 March

An injection of much-needed fresh-start fire as the astrological year begins anew.

SPRING EQUINOX
20 March

As day and night become equal, it's a great time to take stock and step outside your comfort zone.

MARS ENTERS PISCES
22 March

Putting others' needs before our own can go too far during Mars in Pisces.

FULL MOON ECLIPSE IN LIBRA
25 March

Emotional reveals impacting our closest relationships await.

NO RETROGRADES

SUNDAY
10
March
2024

NEW MOON IN PISCES

London 09:00 | New York 05:00 | Los Angeles 01:00 | Tokyo 18:00 | Sydney 20:00

A super new moon in Pisces offers up a peaceful path to progress that's more about going with the flow than grasping for more. The final sign of the zodiac, Pisces knows the true value of an ending is the fresh start it leaves in its wake, which makes this the perfect new moon to believe in the possibility of a dream come true. Think fantasies made reality, meaningful intuitive downloads and soaking up the magic of life in the slow lane.

NEW MOON INTENTIONS FOR YOUR SIGN

Go with the flow this new moon

ARIES	♈	Forgive someone you might rather forget.
TAURUS	♉	Don't be afraid to ask for help from a new or old connection.
GEMINI	♊	Set your sights on a serious work goal and start making it happen.
CANCER	♋	Make a bucket list of travel intentions for the future.
LEO	♌	Accept an offer of financial help and make it count.
VIRGO	♍	Put someone else's needs before yours in a romance.
LIBRA	♎	Leave an unhealthy habit behind as you invite vitality and wellbeing into your life.
SCORPIO	♏	Step into the spotlight like the star that you are.
SAGITTARIUS	♐	Celebrate your chosen family as much as the one you were born into.
CAPRICORN	♑	Have an overdue heart-to-heart before it's too late.
AQUARIUS	♒	Aim for a financial upgrade and don't stop until you've hit the jackpot.
PISCES	♓	Shake off the self-doubt and start owning your magic.

MONDAY
25
March
2024

FULL MOON ECLIPSE IN LIBRA

London 07:00 | New York 03:00 | Los Angeles 00:00 | Tokyo 16:00 | Sydney 18:00

The March Worm Moon kicks off eclipse season (for more on this, see p74–9) in peace-seeking Libra inviting all of us to consider the ways in which we relate to others. Dynamic duos of all kinds fall into focus with Libra at the helm so anyone looking to level up a romance or seek closure on a past hurt should get ready to tune in to the power of this lunation. Expect big feelings, big eclipse realizations and, if you're lucky, a touch of romance.

FULL MOON THEMES & QUESTIONS FOR YOUR SIGN

		THEMES	ASK YOURSELF
ARIES	♈	Romance, duos, teaming up with someone else in life or love	*How is my past impacting my hopes for the future?*
TAURUS	♉	Mental wellbeing, physical health, feeling the need to reboot your life	*What can I add to my life to help me feel more energized?*
GEMINI	♊	All eyes on you, endless invitations, something to celebrate, a new addition	*What do I need to feel ready to show up fully in my life?*
CANCER	♋	Getting a house in order, friends who feel like family, leaving your old life behind	*How best can I create a stable foundation for myself?*
LEO	♌	Being asked your opinion, sharing a big idea with the world, finding your voice	*Who really needs to hear what I have to say?*
VIRGO	♍	Learning to put yourself first, pushing for a better deal, receiving a big payoff	*How can I boost my self-worth?*

Attune to the magic of the Libra full moon

	THEMES	ASK YOURSELF
LIBRA ♎	Feeling ready for change, thinking about what you really want out of life	*If I knew I couldn't fail what would I do next?*
SCORPIO ♏	Getting comfortable with your shadows, healing old wounds, forgiving someone	*How can I create more time for the things that make me feel good?*
SAGITTARIUS ♐	Joining a new group or community, making friends, fighting for justice	*How can I contribute to the greater good?*
CAPRICORN ♑	Changing your job or career, understanding what success means to you	*Where do I really want to be in five years' time?*
AQUARIUS ♒	Exploring new ideas, leaving one interest behind to concentrate on another, travel	*What would make my life feel full of potential right now?*
PISCES ♓	Focusing in on a passion project, feeling consumed by a romance, dangerous liaisons	*Am I in too deep with something I might regret?*

DIVE DEEPER 2024:
ECLIPSE SEASON

Eclipse season is a cosmic wild card offering up reboots, revelations, shake-ups and switch-ups. Eclipses are either lunar (where the earth is between the sun and the full moon, blocking the reflection of light onto the moon's surface) or solar (where the new moon is between the earth and the sun, blocking the sun's light) and always come in pairs. There are two (rarely three) annual eclipse periods each year and while we can't always see them – depending on their path, timing and cloud cover – we can often feel their cosmic effects.

Astrologically, eclipses activate the lunar nodes (north and south nodes, known as the nodes of fate) and the pair of signs those nodes are currently in. The nodes change signs every eighteen months and you're more likely to feel the impact of eclipse season if they're in your sign. This year that means Libra and Aries will be feeling the impact of eclipses the most (a cycle that began in April 2023), followed by Pisces and Virgo whose eclipse cycle begins on 18 September (and follows through into 2026). That said, anyone can find themselves impacted by eclipse season depending on their individual birth chart and cosmic sensitivity!

Eclipses are said to usher in change, sudden realizations and new ways of understand the world and how we relate to it. There's a sense that whatever rises to the surface during an eclipse is something you need to know to move forwards. As tempting as it is to get on with your usual new moon intentions and full moon manifesting rituals during an eclipse, there's often more magic to be found in sitting back and waiting to see what comes up.

All eclipses are cosmic wild cards but generally speaking a solar eclipse (which occurs during a new moon) tends to hammer home the need for a new beginning (sometimes by slamming a door in your face), while a lunar eclipse (which occurs during a full moon) is more of an emotional cosmic big reveal, shining a sudden, shocking spotlight on what's no longer working. Put it this way, if the love of your life has been cheating on you, you'll probably find out on a lunar eclipse.

THE ECLIPSES OF 2024

See also the new and full moon pages in the relevant months for guidance specific to your sign.

Monday
25
March
2024

LUNAR ECLIPSE IN LIBRA (PENUMBRAL)

Eclipse season 2024 kicks off with a lunar eclipse in relationship-focused Libra.

THE VIBE

This eclipse offers up a few home truths when it comes to our closest relationships. Perhaps you've been taking more than you give? Perhaps someone's intentions aren't quite what they seem? Maybe a wake-up call is long overdue? This full moon eclipse in Libra could bring some big feelings and important questions to the surface.

THE VISION

This eclipse is penumbral, which occurs when the moon travels through the earth's shadow, making it appear slightly darker. Penumbral eclipses are difficult to see with the naked eye but if you live in North or South America and pay close attention (the effect is a very slight darkening of the moon) you might just catch it.

THE RITUAL

Self-love is the gateway to true love this full moon eclipse. Take time out to meditate, read, relax, journal or give yourself a makeover. Skip any manifestation rituals and simply allow whatever is coming through for you to bubble up and make itself known. Slip a piece of rose quartz under your pillow for added magic.

MONDAY
8
April
2024

SOLAR ECLIPSE IN ARIES (TOTAL)

The second eclipse this season is a big one: a total solar eclipse in fiery Aries.

THE VIBE

Brace yourself for a next-level awakening, revelation or sudden change. There's an intensity to this solar eclipse – partly as a result of the planetary pile-up surrounding it and partly because everyone is talking about it! – that might feel too hot to handle at times. Taking place in fiery Aries, this eclipse invites us to face our shadows, choose the most authentic path forwards and be who we really are.

THE VISION

Set to be the most-watched celestial event in history, this total eclipse of the sun will be at least partially visible across much of North America. It will be visible in its totality in a path populated by over 30 million people, covering the coast of Mexico, Austin, Dallas, Buffalo and Montreal (as well as all over the Internet).

THE RITUAL

Try a candle meditation to help you focus, look within and tune in to the messages and revelations of this total eclipse. Light a candle (red for passion, white for fresh starts, green for luck and abundance), try some journalling using the prompt 'Because I am free to be my true self I...' and see what comes up for you. When you feel ready, gaze into the flame of the candle and invite the message you need most to come to you. Extinguish the flame at the moment of the eclipse for extra magic.

Wednesday
18
September
2024

LUNAR ECLIPSE IN PISCES (PARTIAL)

Next up is a lunar eclipse in dreamy Pisces.

THE VIBE

Mystical Pisces brings all the big feels to eclipse season, making this full super moon a powerful time to heal a past hurt or seek closure. We all have things we need to leave behind if we want to move forwards in life and this eclipse is here to show us the way. It might not feel that way at first but an ending that breaks your heart now could become the brightest new beginning.

THE VISION

As long as the clouds play ball you should be able to catch a glimpse of this partial lunar eclipse from North and South America, Africa and most of Europe. Be warned it won't be the most dramatic viewing experience as just a small portion of the moon will be covered by the sun!

THE RITUAL

A full moon eclipse (partial) in Pisces calls for a bath ritual. Fill the tub (you can use a shower if you don't have a bath), go to town on candles and fragrant oils, indulge in a soak and visualize what you wish to release going down the plughole with the water at the end. Finish with some outdoor moonbathing for extra power.

Wednesday
2
October
2024

SOLAR ECLIPSE IN LIBRA (ANNULAR)

The final eclipse of 2024 is in peace-seeking Libra.

THE VIBE

Relationships of all kinds fall into focus during this eclipse. There's a sense that any secrets or shadows need to come to the surface now, ushering in a new era of truth and authenticity. Expect endings, expect beginnings, expect sudden heartfelt feelings you can't possibly deny. Could it be that the partnership you've been dreaming of was right in front of you all along?

THE VISION

Annular eclipses occur when the new moon covers the sun's centre, leaving a ring-of-fire effect visible from Earth. For those lucky enough to live in the direct path of this eclipse - parts of southern Chile, Argentina and Easter Island - the effect should be pretty impressive. A partial view is possible across much of South America, the Pacific, parts of the Atlantic and Antarctica, depending on sky conditions.

THE RITUAL

There's power in connection for this new moon eclipse so try not to go it alone. Get a friend, family member or lover on board to join you in a new moon meditation. Take it in turns to speak from the heart, voicing everything you wish for and everything you wish to let go of. As with all eclipse rituals don't try to force anything, just allow whatever is rising within you to come to the surface. Try a DIY tarot reading for magical insights.

APRIL

ARIES SEASON

♈

Welcome to Aries Season 82
Aries 83
Tune in to Aries Season 84
Starstruck: Earth Day 85
Aries Season for Your Sign 86
Key Cosmic Dates 88
Dive Deeper 2024:
    Mercury Retrograde 90
    Mercury Retrogrades of 2024 92
New Moon Eclipse in Aries 94
Full Moon in Scorpio 96

WELCOME TO ARIES SEASON

Ready to shake things up, fuel your inner fire and smash a few goals? Aries season has enough devil-may-care attitude to kick anyone out of their comfort zone. The fast-paced fire of previous Aprils may be slightly tempered this year due to eclipse season and Mercury retrograde (see p74–9 and p90–3) but even the mistiest cosmic weather is no match for the ram on a mission.

If you have an Aries in your life, you'll know about it – and you're probably struggling to keep up! Dynamic and innovative, the first sign of the zodiac moves fast, talks fast and gets bored fast, leaving a trail of brilliant but unfinished projects, plans and ideas in their wake. As careless as this sounds, there's something special about Aries' ability to quit while they're ahead. We can all learn something from the way this sign follows their heart without worrying about what anyone else thinks.

This fiery ram's lust for life, thrills and new adventures make them a total blast to hang out with. If you're meeting for drinks in the hottest new bar, three days before it officially opens, you can bet Aries had a hand in the planning. This is a sign that thrills in living in the moment.

Aries is brave, bold and a master of reinvention, always ready to go first, dive in at the deep end and tell it like it is. Unashamedly and outrageously themselves, Aries is passionate, powerful and authentic. Fancy what they're having? Invest in yourself, believe you have something unique to offer the world and make like the main character you know you were born to be.

ARIES

20 March–18 April

THE REBEL - *Fiery. Feisty. Fast-paced. First.*

SYMBOL	Ram
RULED BY	Mars
ELEMENT	Fire
MODALITY	Cardinal
RULES THE	1st House of Self, Image, Identity & Personality
LUCKY DAY	Tuesday
STAR STONE	Bloodstone
SOUL FLOWER	Thistle
AT THEIR BEST	Brave, pioneering, energetic
AT THEIR WORST	Angry, selfish, over-competitive
TAROT CARD	The Emperor

ARIES 101

VIBE	In it to win it, dynamic force of nature
STYLE	Fashion forward, bold statements, colour blocking, giant sunglasses, hats with everything, show-stopping accessories
LOVES	Competition
HATES	To lose
MOST LIKELY TO	Predict the next big thing
JUST DON'T	Expect them to wait in line
FIND THEM	Powerwalking, first in line, running the show, leaving unfinished business in their wake
BORN TO	Act now, think later

TUNE IN TO ARIES SEASON

Get fired up for the astrological New Year

START SOMETHING NEW Aries is more of a starter than a finisher (all the new directions, all the time!) and this sign's ability to set wheels in motion is second to none. If you've got an idea on the back-burner, Aries season is a great time to let it see the light of day.

LEVEL UP YOUR LOOK Aries loves to use personal style to transform the way they feel. If you're ready to upgrade your look, stand out from the crowd and become more YOU than ever, now is the time.

SEE THE BIGGER PICTURE Zoom out, stress less and ask yourself how much the details really matter. As long as you get where you need to be in the end, does it matter if the journey isn't perfect?

LEAD THE WAY Natural-born leader Aries has courage and conviction. If you have a passion, a mission or a desire to disrupt the status quo, now might be a good time take the lead.

FEEL THE FEAR AND DO IT ANYWAY No one leaps head first into life like Aries. Tune in to this by facing a fear and stepping outside your comfort zone and see what magic awaits.

MAKE LIKE THE MAIN CHARACTER Aries energy is so main character it's probably getting its own spin-off show. Romanticize your life, dress to impress and gaze dramatically into the middle distance so everyone knows how central you are.

If life feels more fizzle than fire right now, it's not you, it's Mercury retrograde. *See p90–3.*

STARSTRUCK

EARTH DAY

22 April

Earth Day marks the anniversary of the birth of the modern environmental movement and highlights the importance of environmental consciousness. Ushered in by earth sign Taurus this is the ideal time astrologically to get grounded, appreciate the beauty of the natural world and take steps towards protecting our environment.

CELEBRATE THE EARTH

FIRE SIGNS	*Aries* *Leo* *Sagittarius*	High-energy fire signs are brilliant at getting people's attention. Try turning your anger at the state of the world into action by leading a protest, starting a campaign and calling out bad practice where you see it.
EARTH SIGNS	*Taurus* *Virgo* *Capricorn*	Taking care of the world comes naturally to earth signs. And action speaks louder than words. Encourage others to care for the environment by leading by example, getting your hands dirty with a community garden project and supporting grassroots environmental initiatives.
AIR SIGNS	*Gemini* *Libra* *Aquarius*	Charming and persuasive air signs were born to change minds, fight injustice and bring game-changing ideas. Allow your creativity to solve old problems in new ways, challenge the norm and talk everyone into going plant-based.
WATER SIGNS	*Cancer* *Scorpio* *Pisces*	It's all about the H2O for sensitive water sign souls. Channel big feelings into saving seas, cleaning up oceans and making our rivers a healthy environment for wildlife. Ditch the plastic, use public transport and join a beach clean-up to do your bit.

ARIES SEASON FOR YOUR SIGN

♈ ARIES Bring out the big guns for birthday season. Revamp your look, rethink your life goals and showcase the new you for the world.

If you do one thing this month: Make plans.

♉ TAURUS A long overdue break is on the cards for you this month. Taking time out to prioritize your mind, body and soul could prove life-changing.

If you do one thing this month: Take some recovery time.

♊ GEMINI Accepting the changing nature of a friendship that matters to you could feel overwhelming this month. Embrace the shift and you might find new common ground.

If you do one thing this month: Allow others to change as much as you do.

♋ CANCER If the success you crave feels just out of reach this might be the month to change tack. Contemplate your options and think again when it comes to a big goal because there might be another way to get there.

If you do one thing this month: Pivot your thinking.

♌ LEO Cancelled travel plans, passport issues or work commitments could see you grounded when you want to fly this month. Double-check everything and try again.

If you do one thing this month: Read the small print.

♍ VIRGO A high stress month might see you showing your dark side. Pay attention to those who see you at your worst and love you anyway.

If you do one thing this month: Be ready to apologize.

♎ LIBRA Desperate to level up in a relationship? This could be a tricky month for progress but an important one for reassessing your options and deciding what matters most to you.

If you do one thing this month: Be patient.

♏ SCORPIO One step forwards, two steps back with a health kick you know could change your life forever? Cut yourself some slack this month but lay the groundwork for future success.

If you do one thing this month: Schedule time to prioritize your wellbeing.

♐ SAGITTARIUS An old project or forgotten passion you rediscover this Aries season could hold the key to future success. Dig out your diaries, finish the desk drawer novel and start creating something again.

If you do one thing this month: Believe in second chances.

♑ CAPRICORN Allowing yourself to revisit a home or family decision made earlier in the year to see if it still works for you could be the wake-up call you need most this month.

If you do one thing this month: Don't rush it.

♒ AQUARIUS Think before you speak this Aries season, Aquarius. You have something important to share with the world but the world may not be ready to hear it just yet. Hold out a little longer and you'll be better placed to get the results you want.

If you do one thing this month: Think first, act later.

♓ PISCES It's about time you reaped some of the rewards of a job well done, Pisces, but it seems the cosmos didn't get the memo this month. Keep the faith. Your time is coming.

If you do one thing this month: Spend within your means.

APRIL

Key Cosmic Dates

MERCURY RETROGRADE BEGINS *1 April*	The messenger planet's backspin in fiery Aries tempers the fire sign's usual high energy with a slower pace.
VENUS ENTERS ARIES *5 April*	Less talk more action is the motto of Venus in Aries. Just take care to say what you mean and mean what you say while Mercury remains retrograde.
NEW MOON ECLIPSE IN ARIES *8 April*	The celestial event of the year is here (see p94–5). A super new moon total solar eclipse in Aries brings fire, passion and the right kind of change into our lives.
TAURUS SEASON BEGINS *19 April*	Earthy, reliable, indulgent Taurus invites us to make progress on a goal, believe in ourselves and save nothing for best.
FULL MOON IN SCORPIO *24 April*	Expect heightened emotions and intuitive nudges at the Scorpio full moon. Transformation awaits!
MERCURY RETROGRADE ENDS *25 April*	Breathe a sigh of relief as direct motion resumes. Life should start to feel like it's progressing again soon.
MARS ENTERS ARIES *30 April*	The fresh-start energy we've been waiting for all month arrives to fire things up.

RETROGRADE (RX) PLANETS

MERCURY RX

1–25 April
(in Aries)

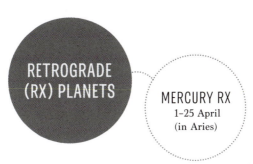

DIVE DEEPER 2024:

MERCURY RETROGRADE

1–2 January | 1–25 April | 5–28 August | 26 November–15 December

HOW TO HANDLE THE MESSENGER PLANET'S BACKSPIN

Take the astro memes literally and you could be forgiven for thinking that Mercury retrograde is the harbinger of doom, disaster and endless tech fails. The list of things you supposedly 'shouldn't do' during the messenger planet's backspin – sign contracts, start new projects, buy electrical goods – is enough to make you wonder if you should hide under a rock until it's over. The truth, though, is that it's not all bad!

Mercury isn't the only planet in the solar system that spends time in retrograde, it just gets all the attention because it happens the most often, usually three times a year, for three weeks at a time. And while the backwards movement is in fact an optical illusion, the effects can feel very real.

The social media hot takes might be OTT – life can't just stop for nine weeks of the year! – but if your Wifi's gone down, your train's cancelled and you've lost all your passwords it might be worth checking what's going on in the cosmos. Mercury retrograde can send aspects of our lives connected to communication and travel into freefall but if you know what you're dealing with it can also be a brilliantly restorative time to slow down and hit the reset button. A Mercury backspin invites us to take our time, press pause and see the bigger picture.

If you find yourself dreading Mercury retrograde it might be time to reframe it as an opportunity to take stock, rethink things and make sure the path you're following is the right one for you. Read on for tips on how to make the most of Mercury retrograde.

BE BORN READY	Travel delays and tech troubles are no big deal if you're prepared. Double-check details, download a podcast in case you get stuck somewhere and make sure your passport is up to date.
GO SLOW	There's no better time to live life in the slow lane than during a Mercury backspin. Take a few days off if you can and turn off your phone. It's the perfect time for peace, reflection and a total digital detox.
RETHINK, REDO, REVISIT	Avoiding all new projects during Mercury retrograde is obviously impossible but it is an excellent time to revisit an old one. Mercury retrograde is an ideal time to consider your options, give a project a second chance or finish something you started a while back.
EXPECT A TEXT FROM YOUR EX	There's a nostalgic, trickster side to Mercury that creates prime conditions for dodgy exes to slide into your DMs. It's not you, it's Mercury - don't fall for the same cheap lines this time around.
WATCH YOUR WORDS	Misunderstandings can feel rife during Mercury retrograde so think twice before you fire off that angry email, confront a friend or post the pictures from last night on Instagram. Choose your words carefully to avoid drama!

MERCURY RETROGRADES OF 2024

Understand that Mercury retrograde (when the planet appears to be moving backwards in the sky) is more of an invitation to press pause, reset and reconsider than the overwhelming disaster the astro memes would have you believe and it can actually become something to look forward to.

Yes, life can feel a bit up in the air while the messenger planet takes its annual backspins but there's really no reason to let it stop you getting on and enjoying life (see p124 for tips on how to handle them). That said, it's worth knowing when it's happening and in what sign so you can be prepared for potential miscommunications, delays and slower progress on projects and plans.

Retrogrades also have a shadow period that means their impact can sometimes be felt before they start or after they finish. So if you're still feeling it when it's meant to be over, it's not you, it's the cosmos.

1–2 January

MERCURY RETROGRADE IN SAGITTARIUS

Honesty isn't always the best policy (no matter what straight-talking Sagittarius would have us believe) – a little tact could go along way this New Year! Try not to take offence too easily, either – misunderstandings and miscommunications could definitely feature as 2024 begins.

This retrograde is also well-timed for a bit of New Year reflection. Revisiting an abandoned project, course of study or travel plan could prove a fruitful way to start 2024.

1-25 April — MERCURY RETROGRADE IN ARIES

Life might feel frustratingly on hold during this retrograde so be prepared to work on projects behind the scenes as April begins. Have faith that your big reveal is still on track for success and might even turn out better thanks to the extra planning time.

Calm is key during this retrograde, as is trying to listen more than you talk. It's also a really good time to work on yourself and spend time back at the drawing board of big life overhauls and decisions.

5-28 August — MERCURY RETROGRADE IN VIRGO (5–15 AUGUST) & LEO (15–28 AUGUST)

The struggle is real with Mercury retrograde in Virgo. Delays, tech issues and missed appointments could all feature so try to double-check dates and have a book, podcast and spare charger with you so you can make the most of any waiting time.

When the retrograde shifts into Leo midmonth, delays could become the least of your worries. Mercury retrograde loves a blast from the past, and Leo loves a dramatic flirtation, so don't be surprised to find a wayward ex or two sliding into your DMs. The answer is still 'No', right?

26 November–15 December — MERCURY RETROGRADE IN SAGITTARIUS

We end the year as we started it with Mercury retrograde in optimistic, globe-trotting Sagittarius. Once again, taking care to avoid misunderstandings could be key during this time, as well as being prepared for travel plans to stall or change.

This change is perfectly timed for anyone ready to spend time reflecting on how they've grown and evolved over the year. Beginning to gently make plans for the future while tying up loose ends from 2024 could be a really valuable way to spend this backspin – which handily ends in time for the festive season!

MONDAY
8
April
2024

NEW MOON ECLIPSE IN ARIES

London 19:21 | New York 14:21 | Los Angeles 11:21 | Tokyo 03:21 9 April | Sydney 04:21 9 April

It's all eyes skywards this super new moon, with a dramatic total eclipse of the sun visible across much of North America and Mexico in the early afternoon. While new moons are usually prime times for thinking big and setting intentions, eclipses lend themselves to more inward-looking spiritual practices. That doesn't mean you can't write a wish list to the universe if you want to but it does mean there's magic to be found in slowing down and seeing what comes up for you as the sky goes dark (even if you only witness it on your computer screen). This new moon is in fiery, forward-thinking Aries, inviting us to consider the ways in which we innovate, push forwards and face the world. For more on eclipse season, see p74–9.

ECLIPSE SEASON

NEW MOON ECLIPSE REVEALS FOR YOUR SIGN

Take a break from intention setting this new moon

ARIES	♈	Something that's been building for a long time is about to become real for you.
TAURUS	♉	Allow your intuition to lead you down a magical path to closure.
GEMINI	♊	False friends could show their true colours this new moon. Watch and wait.
CANCER	♋	The answer to a tricky work or career dilemma could be closer than you think.
LEO	♌	A bright idea or new obsession could change your perspective this new moon eclipse.
VIRGO	♍	An opportunity for a life less conventional is about to reveal itself to you.
LIBRA	♎	Expect a big realization about your work-life balance as you learn the importance of putting yourself first.
SCORPIO	♏	Pay attention to a health or wellbeing wake-up call – it's more important than you realize.
SAGITTARIUS	♐	A potentially life-changing offer could be headed your way soon. Be ready to do what feels right.
CAPRICORN	♑	A family surprise that changes your plans for the future may be about to rock your world.
AQUARIUS	♒	The thrill of a truth revealed could be your first step to freedom.
PISCES	♓	Be ready to feel the fear and do it anyway as this eclipse reveals the magic you have to offer the world.

WEDNESDAY
24
April
2024

FULL MOON IN SCORPIO

London 00:49 | New York 19:49 23 April | Los Angeles 16:49 23 April | Tokyo 08:49 | Sydney 09:49

April's Pink Moon falls in intense, mysterious Scorpio, sign of transformation, secrets and next-level intuition. This makes it a great lunation to consider how we can listen to our intuition more and trust what it tells us. What niggling doubt have you been pushing to the back of your mind? What is trying to get your attention? What do you need to wave goodbye to now if you want to truly step into your power?

FULL MOON THEMES & QUESTIONS FOR YOUR SIGN

	THEMES	ASK YOURSELF
ARIES ♈	Making big changes to the way you live your life, an intense personal transformation	*What – if anything – is holding me back from stepping into this new version of myself?*
TAURUS ♉	Partnerships, relationships, double acts, putting someone else's needs before your own	*How can I prioritize the people who matter most?*
GEMINI ♊	A change in routine, getting up earlier, feeling inspired to exercise, a health kick	*What does work-life balance really mean to me?*
CANCER ♋	Fun times, party invitations, rediscovering a childhood passion, love at first swipe	*How can I do more of the things that bring me joy?*
LEO ♌	Starting a renovation, browsing property websites, moving in with someone, escaping a tricky family dynamic	*What cycles need to be broken for me to live freely?*

Attune to the magic of the Scorpio full moon

		THEMES	ASK YOURSELF
VIRGO	♍	Sharing your story, a new writing or speaking project, telling the truth, taking a short trip somewhere	*How can my story help others?*
LIBRA	♎	Knowing your worth, building up your self-esteem, expecting better, refusing to settle	*How can I aim higher in all areas of my life?*
SCORPIO	♏	Showing a hidden side of yourself, living your truth, changing your physical appearance	*What can I do today that I've been putting off for too long?*
SAGITTARIUS	♐	Spending time alone, discovering a spiritual practice, prioritizing sleep, forgiving someone who hurt you	*How can I create more space for rest in my life?*
CAPRICORN	♑	Finding your people, joining a club, creating an online community, fighting for a cause	*What limiting belief is stopping me from making a dream reality?*
AQUARIUS	♒	Career developments, signing on the dotted line, becoming part of a power couple, letting go of a dream	*Will this opportunity really help me get to where I want to go?*
PISCES	♓	Big plans, big thinking, studying something that fascinates you, being honest with someone, making travel plans	*Why would I let anything get in my way this time?*

MAY

TAURUS SEASON

♉

Welcome to Taurus Season **100**
Taurus **101**
Tune in to Taurus Season **102**
Starstruck: Beltane **103**
Taurus Season for Your Sign **104**
Key Cosmic Dates **106**
New Moon in Taurus **108**
Full Moon in Sagittarius **110**
Dive Deeper 2024:
Jupiter in Gemini **112**

WELCOME TO TAURUS SEASON

Slow and steady wins the race when Taurus is running the show. As spring peaks, the zodiac's dependable and devoted pleasure-seeker ushers in a relaxed easy-living vibe that invites all of us to stop and smell the roses.

Taurus is a sign that values stability, security, relaxation and luxury. To put it simply: they like things nice. Yes, Taurus can be a dedicated and hard-working force of nature but if they could spend the rest of their days dressed in head-to-toe cashmere, flitting between spa breaks and Michelin-starred restaurants, they definitely would. Happiest off-grid and surrounded by nature, Taurus is all in when it comes to good food, fine wine and unapologetic indulgence. There's no such thing as 'saving for best' when Taurus is in charge.

Taurus knows what they like and likes what they know, so they can find change confronting. While this might come across as an infuriating stubborn streak - sorry, bulls, but the clichés are true with this one - there's a pleasing flipside to this sign's inflexible nature. When Taurus is committed they're really committed. Loyal, loving and totally trustworthy, if you've bagged a Taurean lover, business partner or BFF you've got them for the long haul.

This sign's love of the good life means financial security is important to them and they're not afraid to put in the work required to achieve it. Providers, builders and creators, Taurean's are the zodiac's architects, forever on a mission to stabilize their foundations, create beauty in the world and grow something wonderful from the ground up.

When it all comes good for Taurus - as eventually it always does - there's no scrimping on the celebrations, either: luxury all the way. Spend some time languishing in Taurus world and you'll never want to leave.

TAURUS

19 April–19 May

THE ROCK - *Grounded. Reliable. Loyal. Classy.*

SYMBOL	Bull
RULED BY	Venus
ELEMENT	Earth
MODALITY	Fixed
RULES THE	2nd House of Wealth, Values & Possessions
LUCKY DAY	Friday
STAR STONE	Emerald
SOUL FLOWER	Rose
AT THEIR BEST	Trustworthy, protective, extravagant, sensual
AT THEIR WORST	Stubborn, lazy, inflexible, cautious
TAROT CARD	The Hierophant

TAURUS 101

VIBE	Romantic ride or die with a penchant for self-care
STYLE	Heritage labels, cosy knits, luxe fabrics, future heirlooms
LOVES	The good life
HATES	Change
MOST LIKELY TO	To achieve any goal they set their mind to
JUST DON'T	Expect them to slum it
FIND THEM	Having a lie in, at a spa, eating out, building a business, hiding out in a cabin in the woods
BORN TO	Luxuriate

TUNE IN TO TAURUS SEASON

Get grounded this May

SLOW DOWN It's time to embrace life in the slow lane, go the long way round, stop for a chat, take your time and quit rushing. Taurus knows the best things come to those who wait so press pause, look around you and soak it all in.

EXPECT MORE There's no settling for second best in Taurus season. This is the perfect month to practise asking for more, investing in the good stuff and knowing your worth.

STAY IN YOUR COMFORT ZONE Not everything in life has to be a bold, brave leap into the unknown. Get reacquainted with your comfort zone this Taurus season! Think long chats with old friends, ordering your usual, classic films and nostalgic tunes.

GET OUTSIDE Everything feels better outside of four walls. Take yourself to the great outdoors, sit with the sun on your face, walk barefoot on the earth and notice the beauty that surrounds you.

INDULGE Taurus season is all about pleasure seeking so pick your indulgence and go all in. Spa days, massages, tasting menus, expensive candles and silk pyjamas all bring maximum Taurus vibes.

CHILL OUT Taking time out to rest and relax is how Taurus stays grounded while the rest of us are losing the plot. Take a nap, schedule a siesta or just cut yourself some slack while the spring sun shines.

PRIORITIZE YOUR MENTAL HEALTH If your own oxygen mask is always the last thing on your mind, it's time to ring the changes. Taking time for your own mental health and wellbeing is the kind of Taurus season investment we can all benefit from.

STARSTRUCK BELTANE

1 May

Beltane (or May Day) falls between the spring equinox and summer solstice marking the coming of summer. Traditionally celebrated with bonfires and maypoles, fetes and feasting, this ancient fire festival is a celebration of freedom, fun and long summer days ahead. It's the ideal time to practise gratitude, commune with nature and notice the abundance all around us.

CELEBRATE BELTANE

FLOWER POWER

Create and wear a beautiful flower crown or make a floral wreath for your front door. Leaving small posies of flowers on the doorsteps of friends and family is another magical May Day tradition.

PRACTISE GRATITUDE

Take a look around you and celebrate how far you've come and everything you have. This is the ideal time to start a gratitude journal and begin to notice the change that writing one creates in your life.

PAY IT FORWARD

Finding small ways to make the world a better place is a great way to mark this ancient festival. Gift your time to a friend, charity or community group or find practical ways to live a more sustainable life.

ADORN YOURSELF

Get creative with your look, celebrate who you are now and embrace the spirit of the season. Think colourful clothing, bright manicures and accessories galore.

CREATE A FESTIVAL

Invite friends over for a Beltane feast, dance around a bonfire (or at least light some candles) and celebrate the incoming summer.

SPEND TIME OUTSIDE

If you don't have time for a DIY festival try to spend some time outdoors, walking, relaxing or simply stargazing.

TAURUS SEASON FOR YOUR SIGN

♈ **ARIES** Getting others to value your work as much as you do could feel like an uphill struggle this month. Show them you mean business this time.

If you do one thing this month: Price it higher.

♉ **TAURUS** Make time for the things you find most enjoyable and you'll soon find a way to make life feel like one big celebration.

If you do one thing this month: Invest in yourself.

♊ **GEMINI** A lifestyle shift that's felt overwhelming could require you to slow down more than you'd like this month. A break really will do you good.

If you do one thing this month: Seek closure.

♋ **CANCER** Spending time with old friends could be a salve for your soul. Plan the reunion, gather the gang and make like adult life never happened.

If you do one thing this month: Reach out.

♌ **LEO** Expect big news for your career this month – and it's about time. You've always been a changemaker, Leo – enjoy this moment of recognition.

If you do one thing this month: Know you're worth it.

♍ **VIRGO** An exciting travel plan for later in the year could shift your perspective on life in general. Maybe all you needed was something to look forward to, Virgo?

If you do one thing this month: Book the break.

♎ **LIBRA** An intense month sees you embark on a project with life-changing potential. If you're ready to leave the old you behind, the time has come.

If you do one thing this month: Have faith.

♏ **SCORPIO** A romantic declaration could change your world this month as someone special lays their cards on the table. Are you ready to say the ultimate 'Yes'?

If you do one thing this month: Trust your instincts.

♐ **SAGITTARIUS** It's time to get back on track with a health kick that puts your mental health and wellbeing first.

If you do one thing this month: Put yourself first.

♑ **CAPRICORN** Spend less time building someone else's dream and more time building your own and you won't believe the magic you can make this month.

If you do one thing this month: Enjoy life more.

♒ **AQUARIUS** Exciting news related to your home or family situation could shake up your life in the best possible way. It's time to level up, Aquarius.

If you do one thing this month: Embrace growth.

♓ **PISCES** Your words have more power than you realize, Pisces. A story you've shared could reach a very large audience this May.

If you do one thing this month: Enjoy the spotlight.

MAY

Key Cosmic Dates

BELTANE
1 May
The midpoint between the spring equinox and summer solstice celebrates the power of the sun.

PLUTO RETROGRADE BEGINS
2 May
Pluto retrograde urges us to face our personal shadows so prepare for some serious soul-searching (see p127).

NEW MOON IN TAURUS
8 May
A new moon in earthy Taurus reminds us that taking a break can be as valuable as pressing forwards.

MERCURY ENTERS TAURUS
15 May
Fast-paced Mercury and slow-and-steady Taurus help us make light work of getting the job done this May.

GEMINI SEASON BEGINS
20 May

Time to embrace all the big ideas, have all the life-changing conversations and stop being afraid to change your mind.

FULL MOON IN SAGITTARIUS
23 May

This full moon invites us to dream big, make plans and let go of anything that's stopping us from making them happen.

VENUS ENTERS GEMINI
23 May

Love planet Venus in communicative Gemini brings charm, persuasion and perfect chat-up lines to the table this month.

JUPITER ENTERS GEMINI
26 May

Connection and curiosity count while the planet of fortune takes a spin in Gemini. It's time for us all to seek the truth, speak the truth and think outside the box.

RETROGRADE (RX) PLANETS

PLUTO RX

2 May–12 October
(2 May–2 September in Aquarius;
2 September–12 Oct in Capricorn)

WEDNESDAY
8
May
2024

NEW MOON IN TAURUS

London 04:22 | New York 23:22 7 May | Los Angeles 20:22 7 May | Tokyo 12:22 | Sydney 13:22

The Taurus new moon invites us to set intentions that prioritize downtime and wellbeing as much as goals and progress. This is a lunation that asks us what we value most in life and challenges us to fit more of that into our day-to-day. It's a new moon that invites indulgence, investment (especially in ourselves!) and quiet contemplation, so cut yourself some slack and get real about what matters and what doesn't as summer slowly comes into view.

NEW MOON INTENTIONS FOR YOUR SIGN

Expect more & know your worth this new moon

ARIES	♈	Ask yourself how you can aim even higher when it comes to life, wealth and your career.
TAURUS	♉	This is the big one for you! Choose a new path wisely this new moon.
GEMINI	♊	Make finally getting closure on a past hurt your new moon priority.
CANCER	♋	Make a brave move that can open doors into a new world or community.
LEO	♌	Choose an intention that puts levelling up in your career at the top of your To Do list.
VIRGO	♍	Set wheels in motion to make a digital nomad dream reality.
LIBRA	♎	Challenge yourself to face a demon, ask for help or talk it out this new moon.
SCORPIO	♏	You know where you want a relationship to go. Set a goal that lets the object of your desire in on the secret!
SAGITTARIUS	♐	Shake up your daily routine this new moon and the rest of your life will follow suit.
CAPRICORN	♑	Plan a celebration of life, love or a job well done.
AQUARIUS	♒	Plans to relocate, renovate or make a move look lit for you this new moon.
PISCES	♓	Speak a dream into reality. Tell someone what you really want and watch it start to happen.

Thursday
23
May
2024

FULL MOON IN SAGITTARIUS

London 14:53 | New York 09:53 | Los Angeles 06:53 | Tokyo 22:53 | Sydney 23:53

The May Flower Moon falls in expansive, adventurous Sagittarius bringing some summery spirit our way. Associated with long-distance travel, philosophy, learning and education, a Sagittarius full moon is a great time to think bigger when it comes to your plans for the future. If there's somewhere you've always wanted to go or something you've always wanted to learn more about, now might just be the time to make it happen.

FULL MOON THEMES & QUESTIONS FOR YOUR SIGN

	THEMES	ASK YOURSELF
ARIES ♈	Major travel plans, becoming a digital nomad, exploring a subject that fascinates you, telling it like it is, escaping the status quo	*Why can't I have fun all the time?*
TAURUS ♉	A big change or personal transformation, teaming up with someone else financially, unexpected windfalls, intense feelings or obsessions	*Where is my focus needed now?*
GEMINI ♊	Good news in your love life, teaming up for a project, making something more permanent, levelling up in a relationship	*How can I make love an even bigger adventure?*
CANCER ♋	Feeling ready to commit to a health or wellbeing goal, working hard on a project or job, making time for something that matters in your daily routine	*What is my priority goal this summer?*

Attune to the magic of the Sagittarius full moon

	THEMES	ASK YOURSELF
LEO ♌	Planning a celebration, spending time with children, good times, fun, laughter and all the party invitations	*How can I mark and celebrate this stage of my life?*
VIRGO ♍	Finding comfort in the family that you chose, making decisions about the way you want to live, decorating, moving, creating a base	*What do I need to do to break a cycle and create change?*
LIBRA ♎	Braving a heart-to-heart, telling it like it is, hearing someone out, being truthful, embracing change and new ideas	*What parts of myself am I no longer willing to hide?*
SCORPIO ♏	Asking for (or getting!) a pay rise, aiming higher, learning what really matters to you, creating abundance in all areas of your life	*What do I need to say 'No' to now if I truly know my own worth?*
SAGITTARIUS ♐	Making a life-changing decision, finding new ways to express yourself, starting a big adventure, showing the real you to the world	*Who needs to see more of my authentic self?*
CAPRICORN ♑	Taking a break, discovering your spiritual side, forgiving someone, setting yourself free	*What do I need to let go of to move forwards?*
AQUARIUS ♒	Networking opportunities, making connections, finding friendship, a brand new community, standing up for something you believe in	*Are the people around me pushing me forwards or holding me back?*
PISCES ♓	Amazing career news, next-level success, dreams come true, rewards for a job well done	*What is next on my vision board?*

DIVE DEEPER 2024:
JUPITER IN GEMINI

26 May–9 June 2025

It's good vibes all round when the largest and luckiest planet in the solar system takes a spin through your sign – which it does every twelve years – and right now, it's Gemini's turn. The planet of fortune's latest power move is great news for the cosmic twins but you don't have to be a Gemini to feel the magic.

The energy shift created by Jupiter's 26 May move from patient, reliable Taurus into quick-witted, busy Gemini brings all the big ideas to the table. Jupiter in Gemini invites us to expand our minds, escape the bubbles we've found ourselves in and see both sides of the story for once. It's an adventurous, buzzy, change-your-mind kind of vibe – one that eschews binary thinking and embraces open dialogue, while valuing intellect over aesthetics. The truth will out in the best possible way while Jupiter is in Gemini.

Of course, there can be downsides to this kind of energy too. Gemini's easy, breezy curiosity can easily tip over into idea overload and burnout, so choose your focus wisely at this time. No matter how much we want it all and want it now, that just isn't possible if we want to stay grounded. Jupiter's retrograde later in the year (9 October to 4 February 2025) should take the pressure off, bringing some slower introspection our way, but by then your big idea should have already ignited. Whether you choose to fan its growing flames is up to you.

JUPITER IN GEMINI FOR YOUR SIGN

Discover where Jupiter is bringing luck into your life

ARIES ♈ Your luck is in big ideas, important conversations, writing and speaking projects.

TAURUS ♉ Your luck is in a big investment, financial boost or positive change in circumstances.

GEMINI ♊ Your luck is in a new path or big change you've decided to make in your life.

CANCER ♋ Your luck is in finally getting the closure you need to move on with your life.

LEO ♌ Your luck is in an exciting new connection or friendship that leads to a big opportunity.

VIRGO ♍ Your luck is in a career move, recognition for a job well done, awards and accolades.

LIBRA ♎ Your luck is in a trip somewhere exotic, learning something new, exploring some big ideas.

SCORPIO ♏ Your luck is in a personal transformation that changes the way others see you.

SAGITTARIUS ♐ Your luck is in love, romance and partnerships of all kinds.

CAPRICORN ♑ Your luck is in finding a way to make a positive work-life balance a reality.

AQUARIUS ♒ Your luck is in the success of a creative endeavour, parties, celebrations and having a brush with fame.

PISCES ♓ Your luck is in a home or family dream coming true or changing someone's mind on something that matters to you.

JUNE

GEMINI SEASON

Welcome to Gemini Season 116
Gemini 117
Tune in to Gemini Season 118
Starstruck: Summer Solstice 119
Gemini Season for Your Sign 120
Key Cosmic Dates 122
Dive Deeper 2024:
Planetary Retrogrades 124
New Moon in Gemini 128
Full Moon in Capricorn 130

WELCOME TO GEMINI SEASON

Gemini arrives on the scene like a breath of fresh air, all flirty chat, social buzz and non-stop new ideas. In fact, you might want to take a few deep breaths before diving on in to everything this hectic astrological season has to offer. Ready to get out there, make all the plans and do all the things? When the clock strikes Gemini, you're on!

Good times, witty banter and the thrill of the new are all Gemini raisons d'etre. Quick-witted, energetic and clever, Geminis make perfect party guests thanks to their never-ending stream of conversation starters, next-level social skills and captivating charm. Flirtatious, fun and brilliantly persuasive, if you love it when a plan comes together you'll want Gemini on the organizing committee. Hanging out with a twin is a guaranteed blast, just as long as you can find a way to keep up.

This is a sign that gets more than its fair share of negative press and not always without good reason. Gemini can come across as fickle, gossipy or even two-faced at times but – and it's a big but – what can appear to be flippant or manipulative is really just adaptability in overdrive. The Gemini mind works so fast that they can genuinely have a change of opinion between the start of a conversation and the end of it. Seeing both sides of the story comes naturally to this air sign, which is great when you've got a debate on your hands but not much fun when it feels like they're siding with your ex over the break-up.

Busy, bright and always on a mission, there's much to love about this sign's ability to bring people together and make connections count. Keep them interested, switch things up and never give them the silent treatment and you'll have an ally for life in Gemini.

GEMINI

20 May–19 June

THE CHARMER - *Chatty. Quick-witted. Flirtatious. Expressive.*

SYMBOL	Twins
RULED BY	Mercury
ELEMENT	Air
MODALITY	Mutable
RULES THE	3rd House of Communication
LUCKY DAY	Wednesday
STAR STONE	Agate
SOUL FLOWER	Lavender
AT THEIR BEST	Clever, energetic, curious, persuasive
AT THEIR WORST	Fickle, inconsistent, gossipy, chaotic
TAROT CARD	The Lovers

GEMINI 101

VIBE	Fun-loving charmer who never wants to grow up
STYLE	Slogan tees, rainbow brights, clashing prints, new designers, statement accessories
LOVES	A chat
HATES	Feeling stuck in a rut
MOST LIKELY TO	Change their mind
JUST DON'T	Ever give them the silent treatment
FIND THEM	Throwing a party, signing up for an evening class, dancing the night away, flirting with your lover, giving a Ted Talk
BORN TO	Overshare

TUNE IN TO GEMINI SEASON

It's in with the new this June

TALK IT OUT Communication is key in Gemini world. Line up all the heart-to-hearts, soul-searching deep dives and frivolous water-cooler chats while the going is good. If something needs to be said, now is a great time to say it.

TRY SOMETHING NEW The same-old same-old just doesn't cut it with Gemini. They're all in for new experiences, wild ideas and half-baked schemes cooked up at the tail end of raucous nights out. So shake it off, switch things up and do something you've never done before.

EXPAND YOUR MIND Follow your curiosity and see where it takes you. Gemini loves learning, talking and discovering new ways to experience the world. It's a great time to buy the books, go to the seminar or sign up for the workshop!

TURN ON THE CHARM We can all learn something from Gemini's easy charm this season. Strike up conversations in supermarket queues, smile at strangers for no reason and dance like no one is watching.

CHANGE YOUR MIND There nothing wrong with changing your mind as far as Gemini is concerned. If you've been waiting for a good time to turn a 'No' into a 'Yes' or admit you got it wrong, now might just be your moment.

BE SPONTANEOUS Last-minute adventure doesn't have to mean grand plans and long-haul flights for Gemini. Switch things up right where you already are by walking a new route home, ordering takeaway instead of cooking dinner, going to bed early, getting up late or phoning an old friend out of the blue.

STARSTRUCK

SUMMER SOLSTICE

20 June

The summer solstice marks the longest day and shortest night of the year – a time for wild celebration, rituals and magic – as feelings-focused Cancer season begins. Midsummer festivities are all about indulgence, gratitude and appreciating the wonder of the world around us. Remember when you wanted exactly what you have now? Raise a toast to that as the sun rises or sets on one of the year's most magical days.

HOW TO CELEBRATE SOLSTICE

PAY HOMAGE

Summer solstice is a wonderful time to connect with the history of the ground beneath our feet. In the UK, there's nowhere quite like Stonehenge for marking the longest day but, wherever you are in the world, there's magic to be found in local traditions, stories and folklore.

WORSHIP THE SUN

Wherever you are in the world, watching the sun rise (or set if that's easier!) on the longest day is an essential part of any solstice celebration. Make a wish as the sun appears on the horizon (or disappears below it).

EAT, DRINK AND BE MERRY

Gather friends for an outdoor picnic, indulgent feast or wild party. This is the perfect time of year to kick back, share the love and celebrate life.

SET INTENTIONS

As the year reaches its halfway point, reassessing and redefining our 2024 goals is a natural step in the right direction. Harness the potent magic of midsummer with some heartfelt dawn intention setting.

DANCE BY FIRELIGHT

Build a bonfire, spark up the fire pit or just go to town on the candles and sparklers... no solstice celebration is complete without a bit of fiery magic. Write down anything you want to let go of and burn the paper to ash in a heatproof dish before dancing around the flames.

GEMINI SEASON FOR YOUR SIGN

♈ ARIES An important conversation that feels long overdue could switch up your thinking on the future this month. Say what you mean and mean what you say, Aries.

If you do one thing this month: Tell it like it is.

♉ TAURUS If you want to enjoy the finer things in life (and you know you do!) it might be time to make that investment. Take advice but allow your instincts to lead on this one.

If you do one thing this month: Ask for more.

♊ GEMINI Expect a burst of energy when you need it most this month. It's time to follow through on a plan or promise made to yourself before life gets in the way again.

If you do one thing this month: Choose joy.

♋ CANCER If you're finding it harder to forgive and forget than you'd like, this month might show you an unusual solution. Don't look back, you're not going that way.

If you do one thing this month: Let it go.

♌ LEO Time spent with new friends is time well spent this month. A connection you make in your downtime could prove beneficial for a big career move or change in direction.

If you do one thing this month: Swap numbers.

♍ VIRGO The recognition you've been waiting for could finally arrive this month and it feels even more amazing than you imagined. The hard work was worth it, Virgo.

If you do one thing this month: Aim even higher.

♎ LIBRA Find new ways to add adventure to your life without sabotaging a health goal and you'll see the results you want most this month.

If you do one thing this month: Explore more.

♏ SCORPIO An unexpected windfall could change your world for the better as Gemini season hits its stride. Your transformation is almost complete.

If you do one thing this month: Gift yourself.

♐ SAGITTARIUS An exciting new partnership in love or business should help you see the world through fresh eyes this Gemini season. Two heads really are better than one, Sag!

If you do one thing this month: Accept the offer.

♑ CAPRICORN If a plan to seek better work-life balance in 2024 has fallen by the wayside, this is the season to redress the balance.

If you do one thing this month: Lighten up.

♒ AQUARIUS A creative idea you've been pitching for years might finally find its place in the world this month. You don't have to say 'I told you so' but you really were right all along.

If you do one thing this month: Stand out.

♓ PISCES A family member who's felt distant for all the wrong reasons could see the light this Gemini season. Welcome them back with open arms.

If you do one thing this month: Love harder.

JUNE

Key Cosmic Dates

MERCURY ENTERS GEMINI
3 June
Life feels like it's happening in fast-forward with messenger Mercury in social Gemini this June.

NEW MOON IN GEMINI
6 June
A fresh-start new moon in light-hearted, energetic Gemini is the boost we all need this month.

MARS ENTERS TAURUS
9 June
It's eyes on the prize time while passionate Mars takes a spin in steadfast Taurus. Keep working, keep building, keep going and don't stress if it's taking longer than you hoped.

MERCURY ENTERS CANCER
17 June
Let your intuition lead the way while communicative Mercury is in caring, sensitive Cancer. Sometimes heartfelt actions speak louder than words.

VENUS ENTERS CANCER
17 June
Romance is alive and kicking while Venus takes a turn in emotional, nostalgic Cancer. It's a great time to build romantic foundations and get really comfortable with someone you love.

SUN ENTERS CANCER
20 June

Cancer season brings big feelings, nostalgia and romance to the table as summer starts in earnest.

SUMMER SOLSTICE
20 June

The longest day and shortest night is a time to celebrate, make magic and indulge.

FULL MOON IN CAPRICORN
22 June

A full moon in hard-working, driven Capricorn is just what we need to step into a summer of success. It's time to build yourself a high platform so you can reach the stars.

SATURN RETROGRADE BEGINS
29 June

The zodiac's teacher begins its annual backspin offering up the time and space to consolidate lessons learnt earlier in the year. Read all about it on p126.

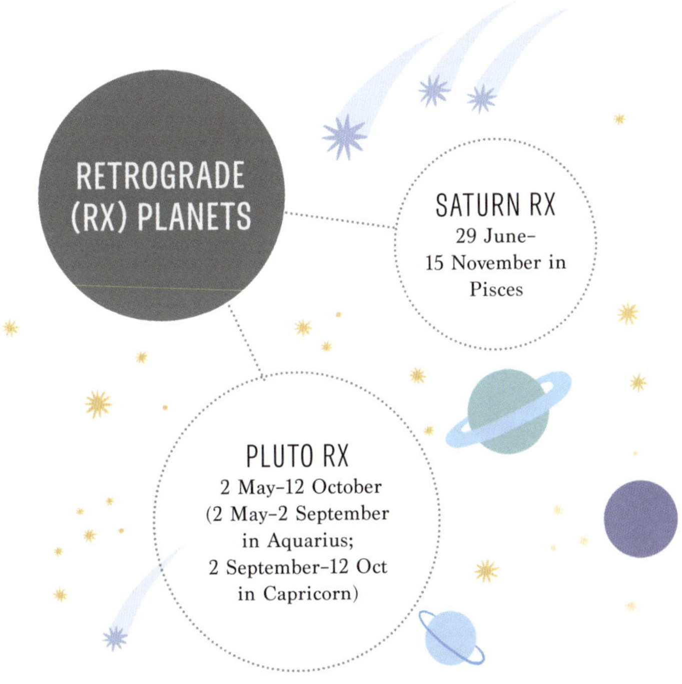

DIVE DEEPER 2024:
PLANETARY RETROGRADES

Mercury might generate all the headlines (read all about it on p90–3) but that doesn't mean it's the only planet with a retrograde worth paying attention to! The rest of the planets all take backspins of their own, some lasting much longer than others, bringing the cosmic shake-ups and slow-downs we need to evolve, grow and initiate change in our lives.

Despite the hype, no retrograde needs to be feared! Some retrogrades last half the year, every year, so putting life on hold is clearly out of the question. There is, however, value in understanding the astrological meaning of each planet's backtrack and how you might make the most of the energy this brings.

Saturn retrograde begins at the end of this month (from 29 June), joining Pluto (which turned retrograde on 2 May) in a backspin through the skies. Read on to discover what this and every planet's retrograde period means.

RETROGRADES 101

HOW TO HANDLE THE BACKSPINS OF 2024

MERCURY THE MESSENGER

1–2 January | 1–25 April | 5–28 August | 26 November–15 December

Mercury is associated with the mind, learning, timing and communication so misunderstandings, miscommunications and slow progress can all be problematic when this planet is retrograde.

HOW OFTEN	Usually three times a year.
HOW LONG	Three weeks at a time.
HOW TO HANDLE IT	Mercury retrograde is best approached as an opportunity to slow down, reassess and revisit your options.

VENUS THE LOVER *No retrograde in 2024*

The planet of love and beauty is associated with style, pleasure and romance. This planet's retrograde can send hearts into free fall as we find ourselves contemplating past loves, questioning commitments and making ill-advised style choices on the fly.

HOW OFTEN Every eighteen months.

HOW LONG Around six weeks.

HOW TO HANDLE IT Focus on self-care and try not to make any rash romantic decisions. This a good time to seek closure on past hurts and show kindness to yourself and others.

MARS THE WARRIOR *6 December 2024–24 February 2025*

Mars brings passion, energy and positive action to the cosmic party, which makes going for our goals and ticking off To Dos feel much harder during its retrograde periods.

HOW OFTEN Around once every two years.

HOW LONG Eight to ten weeks.

HOW TO HANDLE IT Cut yourself some slack, take a break and do as much behind-the-scenes work as possible so you can hit the ground running when Mars is direct again.

JUPITER THE LUCKY CHARM *9 October 2024–4 February 2025*

Expansive, magnanimous Jupiter sprinkles magic dust on everything it touches, filling our worlds with lucky breaks, good fortune and synchronicities. Jupiter's energy is generally outward looking but during its retrograde we are invited to look within, get philosophical and reassess our goals.

HOW OFTEN Once a year.

HOW LONG Around four months.

HOW TO HANDLE IT Time spent soul-searching and tuning in to your own inner wisdom is always time well spent during this retrograde.

SATURN THE TEACHER *29 June–15 November 2024*

Saturn is the taskmaster of the zodiac associated with life lessons, karma and growing up. Saturn likes to make sure we face up to our responsibilities, which means its retrogrades can go both ways, feeling like a pat on the back or a stern telling off depending on which ways we've been adulting lately.

HOW OFTEN Once a year.

HOW LONG Around four and a half months.

HOW TO HANDLE IT This retrograde is the perfect time to tie up loose ends and get real about patterns you're repeating that do not serve you well. It's an opportunity to be honest with yourself about what you need to do to really get your act together.

URANUS THE REBEL *1–27 January 2024 | 1 September 2024–30 January 2025*

The planet of plot twists rules self-awareness, invention and rebellion bringing about collective change and serious shake-ups. During its annual retrograde we often find ourselves forced to confront uncomfortable truths and step out of our comfort zones.

HOW OFTEN Once a year.

HOW LONG Around five months.

HOW TO HANDLE IT Use this time to consider the ways in which you show up in the world and whether you're being true to yourself. If you've been feeling stagnant or stuck now is a good time to get clear about the changes you want to make in your life going forwards.

NEPTUNE THE MYSTIC *2 July–7 December 2024*

Magical mystical Neptune is associated with our hopes and dreams, illusion and intuition. Its annual retrograde can actually be a helpful wake-up call as it invites us to snap out of our fantasy worlds and face up to reality.

HOW OFTEN	Once a year.
HOW LONG	Around five and a half months.
HOW TO HANDLE IT	Be prepared for a revelation that changes how you feel about your relationships, career or life in general. It might not be comfortable – and you definitely don't have to act on it – but a truth revealed in this retrograde could help pave a new path in your life.

PLUTO THE TRANSFORMER *2 May–12 October 2024*

Associated with power, transformation and destruction Pluto rules our shadow selves, subconscious and deepest desires. Life can feel pretty intense during its annual retrograde as we look within and consider the power plays (personal and collective) that are currently impacting our lives.

HOW OFTEN	Once a year.
HOW LONG	Around six months.
HOW TO HANDLE IT	Allow yourself the space and time to really think about what you desire, how you need to change and what steps you must take to get there.

Thursday
6
June
2024

NEW MOON IN GEMINI

London 13:38 | New York 08:38 | Los Angeles 05:38 | Tokyo 21:38 | Sydney 22:38

The fresh-start energy of the new moon is amplified by Gemini's upbeat, positive vibes. If you want to make something happen in your life or turn the beginnings of an idea into magical reality, now is the perfect time to set wheels in motion. Soak up the sense of possibility as you set intentions for the rest of 2024 under this happy-go-lucky new moon.

NEW MOON INTENTIONS FOR YOUR SIGN

Feel inspired by this new moon

ARIES	♈	Speak your truth even if someone doesn't want to hear it.
TAURUS	♉	Make a big investment in your future growth.
GEMINI	♊	It's your personal New Year, Gemini! Make plans that put your needs first.
CANCER	♋	Put an end to something you should have finished a long time ago.
LEO	♌	Make the first move with a group of friends you'd like to spend more time with.
VIRGO	♍	Create a five-year career plan that aims higher than ever before.
LIBRA	♎	Put a date in the diary to start learning more about something you've always been interested in.
SCORPIO	♏	Face up to an uncomfortable truth and find a new way to deal with old ghosts.
SAGITTARIUS	♐	Decide where you want a relationship to go and say 'Yes' when it happens.
CAPRICORN	♑	Tell someone who'll help keep you accountable about a health goal.
AQUARIUS	♒	Explore your creative side in new and interesting ways.
PISCES	♓	Tell the people you love how much you love them.

Saturday
22
June
2024

FULL MOON IN CAPRICORN

London 02:08 | New York 21:08 21 June | Los Angeles 18:08 21 June | Tokyo 10:08 | Sydney 11:08

June's Strawberry Moon falls in ambitious, driven Capricorn urging us to get real about what we need to leave behind to achieve our goals. Capricorn energy is practical and pragmatic so forget dreaming something into existence on manifestation rituals alone. This is a full moon that asks you to shake off the self-doubt so you can take start taking tangible steps towards a new reality. You're good enough, you can do it and it is going to happen.

FULL MOON THEMES & QUESTIONS FOR YOUR SIGN

	THEMES	ASK YOURSELF
ARIES ♈	Big developments in your work or career, winning an award or prize, feeling inspired about the next stage in your life	*What is my biggest dream right now?*
TAURUS ♉	Planning the trip of a lifetime, studying something that interests you, reading around a subject, feeling philosophical about life	*How can I broaden my horizons this summer?*
GEMINI ♊	Being focused on an all-consuming project or person, falling in lust, feeling powerful, getting a cash bonus	*What am I being drawn towards now and why?*
CANCER ♋	Finding a business partnership that works, becoming part of a power couple, making a big commitment, getting married or engaged	*Who makes me want to become a better version of myself?*

Attune to the magic of the Capricorn full moon

	THEMES	ASK YOURSELF
LEO ♌	Getting up earlier, changing your diet, working hard on a personal project, finding new ways to spend your time, nailing it at the gym	*How can I feel my best this summer?*
VIRGO ♍	Going public with a passion project or idea, throwing a party to celebrate your success, spending time with children or young people	*Is it time for me to quit the day job?*
LIBRA ♎	Starting a family, moving house, spending time with people you care about, feeling nostalgic about childhood summers	*What does family mean to me now?*
SCORPIO ♏	Writing about your life, finding a new audience, sharing your soul, planning a staycation, travelling for work (but close to home not long distance)	*Who needs to hear what I have to share?*
SAGITTARIUS ♐	Investing in art, watching your money grow, treating yourself, figuring out what is important to you at work and in life	*What are my core values?*
CAPRICORN ♑	Feeling inspired, embarking on a new project, shaking off old habits that hold you back, feeling lucky	*What truth is being revealed to me now?*
AQUARIUS ♒	Spending time alone, seeking closure, meditating, finding something to believe in	*What do I need to do to better manage my mental health?*
PISCES ♓	Meeting someone who can change your trajectory, finding new friends, starting a community on or offline	*Who am I with when I feel my best?*

JULY

CANCER SEASON

Welcome to Cancer Season 134
Cancer 135
Tune in to Cancer Season 136
Starstruck: Word Power 137
Cancer Season for Your Sign 138
Key Cosmic Dates 140
New Moon in Cancer 142
Full Moon in Capricorn 144

WELCOME TO CANCER SEASON

The zodiac's soft-centered homebody is happiest hibernating on a blanket-laden sofa surrounded by people they love. Creative, sensitive and super-intuitive, feeling feelings is a full-time occupation for this water sign. They don't just focus on their own emotions, either. Cancer is naturally empathetic and likes nothing more than taking care of others, even if it means putting their own needs to the bottom of the pile. Having a Cancerian in your life means never wanting for a shoulder to cry on, a home-cooked meal or someone to put together a tear-jerking slideshow at your next big birthday.

Collecting memories really is important to this nostalgic water sign, so you'll often find them behind the camera, perfecting a retro playlist or gathering friends together for a school reunion. Loyalty knows no bounds for sensitive crabs; once you're in with them, you're in for life - just as long as you play by their rules. Wondering what happens if you cross them? You really don't want to find out!

Do wrong by Cancer and you'll be cast adrift before you've even thought about your first apology message. Confrontation isn't really their vibe but they excel at ghosting and grudges. Your name won't be so much mud as completely buried and forgotten before you've even realized how much you offended them.

Sensitive crabs are natural good Samaritans who make their friends and family central to everything they do. They scrub up like a dream when an event calls for glamour but their idea of real heaven is the buzz and chaos of family and friends gathered around a table in the heart of their home. Cosy up with them on the sofa afterwards and ask if you can flick through their photo albums and they'll probably ask you to move in.

CANCER

20 June–21 July

THE MOONCHILD - *Sensitive. Caring. Intuitive. Creative.*

SYMBOL	Crab
RULED BY	Moon
ELEMENT	Water
MODALITY	Cardinal
RULES THE	4th House of Home, Family & Domesticity
LUCKY DAY	Monday
STAR STONE	Moonstone
SOUL FLOWER	White rose
AT THEIR BEST	Nurturing, creative, empathetic, nostalgic
AT THEIR WORST	Oversensitive, unforgiving, moody, jealous
TAROT CARD	The Chariot

CANCER 101

VIBE	Caring and intuitive empath who knows home is where the heart is
STYLE	Cosy knits, luxe loungewear, cottage-core dresses, event dressing glamour
LOVES	A blast from the past
HATES	Having to get off the sofa
MOST LIKELY TO	Marry their childhood sweetheart
JUST DON'T	Expect to be forgiven if you cross them
FIND THEM	Shopping for blankets, crying over old photos, planning a wedding, cooking a dinner party for twenty-five from scratch
BORN TO	Commit

TUNE IN TO CANCER SEASON

Get cosy this July

CREATE A HAVEN Home is everything for sensitive Cancer souls so spend time making yours a haven. Think a full fridge, clean laundry, twinkly fairylights and an excess of cushions.

FEEL YOUR FEELINGS Cancer wouldn't be Cancer if they weren't weeping over old photos and reminiscing about high school. Let this season be a reminder that it's okay to feel what you feel. Put on a nostalgic playlist and cry it out.

KEEP THINGS SMALL It's all about the inner circle for nurturing Cancer, who prefers to have three or four really good friends over a massive gang. Cosy dinners, couples' cocktails and intimate celebrations with your ride or dies always feel right in Cancer season.

SHOW SOMEONE YOU CARE Caring for others is a big deal in Cancer world so make an effort to show someone how much you care this season. Pick your person and pack their lunch, call them at work, listen to their woes or send them flowers just because.

TAKE A DUVET DAY Escaping the world with a spontaneous duvet day is Cancer's idea of heaven. Stock up on loungewear, old movies and favourite snacks in advance because Cancer also knows it pays to be prepared.

PUT YOURSELF FIRST Cancer's biggest challenge will always be learning to put themselves first so get in there and show them how it's done. Up the self-care, say 'No' when you want to and allow yourself a few indulgences this month.

STARSTRUCK

WORD POWER

We're being urged to get to grips with our dreams for the future this month thanks to a second consecutive full moon in ambitious Capricorn so any tool that offers clarity is a must try. Enter journalling, the practise of free-writing thoughts, feelings and ideas to help process what's going on for us and work out what matters to us most. To start a journalling practice all you need is a pen, paper and some writing time. Many people swear by morning pages - three sheets of flowing stream of consciousness written the moment you wake up - while others love the way prompts send their journal entries in insightful new directions. The thrill of reading back over old entries to discover musings that became magical reality never gets old. Discover the ideal journalling prompt for your sign below.

JOURNALLING PROMPTS FOR YOUR SIGN

Manifest some word power

ARIES ♈ I am who I am meant to be when I...

TAURUS ♉ I have big plans for the future starting with...

GEMINI ♊ I express myself best when I...

CANCER ♋ I feel happiest when...

LEO ♌ I will be living my best life when I...

VIRGO ♍ I make things happen when I...

LIBRA ♎ I balance the different parts of my life by...

SCORPIO ♏ I desire many things but most of all...

SAGITTARIUS ♐ I find adventure when I...

CAPRICORN ♑ I succeed when I...

AQUARIUS ♒ I am free to...

PISCES ♓ I dream that one day...

CANCER SEASON FOR YOUR SIGN

♈ ARIES Pay attention to your foundations as Cancer season hits its stride. You're ready to reach the stars but you also need somewhere solid to land.

If you do one thing this month: Make a house a home.

♉ TAURUS Tell someone how you really feel and you might be pleasantly surprised by their response. A connection that feels right is ready to evolve into something bigger.

If you do one thing this month: Speak your truth.

♊ GEMINI An investment made earlier in the year could begin to pay off this month. The hard work and sacrifice was worth it, Gemini.

If you do one thing this month: Believe your luck.

♋ CANCER It's time for a reboot! Get your life in order, make some summer plans and find a way to prioritize your own goals as the year enters its second half.

If you do one thing this month: Go for gold.

♌ LEO You need a break, Leo, and it's time you actually got round to taking one. Cut yourself some slack so you can truly embrace the next magical stage of your life.

If you do one thing this month: Take a digital detox.

♍ VIRGO A community or group that instantly feels like family could change your world this month. Life really doesn't have to look like the movies.

If you do one thing this month: Let someone in.

♎ LIBRA A payoff or promotion is cause for celebration this Cancer season. Is it time for you to set an even bigger goal?

If you do one thing this month: Accept the praise.

♏ SCORPIO Time spent exploring is time well spent for you this month. Follow your heart and let your intuition guide you to your next big adventure.

If you do one thing this month: Expect the unexpected.

♐ SAGITTARIUS Someone with the capital to invest in your big idea could come good when you need it most this month. Don't wait another minute before you say 'Yes'.

If you do one thing this month: Bet on yourself.

♑ CAPRICORN Taking a step back from a relationship that feels fast-tracked to becoming serious could help you see what you really want, Capricorn. Your true path is about to become clear.

If you do one thing this month: Listen to your heart.

♒ AQUARIUS It's time to ditch an unhealthy habit for good, Aquarius. You know what's good for you, you just need to commit this time.

If you do one thing this month: Change your ways.

♓ PISCES It's your time to shine. Put your best foot forward and embrace an opportunity for all that it is. You've waited a lifetime for a moment like this.

If you do one thing this month: Look your best.

JULY

Key Cosmic Dates

MERCURY ENTERS LEO *2 July*	We all become the drama when Mercury is in Leo. Expect fireworks, fun and flamboyant behaviour.
NEPTUNE RETROGRADE BEGINS *2 July*	Expect wake-up calls and reality checks this retrograde.
NEW MOON IN CANCER *5 July*	A new moon in the sign that's ruled by the moon is a magical way to set intentions.
VENUS ENTERS LEO *11 July*	Love is in the air when Venus is in Leo, inviting all of us to lavish some big-hearted lion energy on our relationships.
MARS ENTERS GEMINI *20 July*	Talking, learning and following our curiosity are themes when Mars is in Gemini. This is a great time for multitasking and expressing ourselves.
FULL MOON IN CAPRICORN *21 July*	A second consecutive full moon in ambitious Capricorn asks us to double down on a big dream and let go of doubt.
LEO SEASON BEGINS *22 July*	Summer doesn't start until the sun comes home to roost in the sunshine sign!
MERCURY ENTERS VIRGO *25 July*	Productive Mercury in Virgo has your back this summer.

RETROGRADE (RX) PLANETS

PLUTO RX
2 May–12 October
(2 May–2 September
in Aquarius;
2 September–12 October
in Capricorn)

SATURN RX
29 June–
15 November in
Pisces

NEPTUNE RX
2 July–
7 December
in Pisces

FRIDAY
5
July
2024

NEW MOON IN CANCER

London 23:57 | New York 18:57 |
Los Angeles 15:57 | Tokyo 07:57 6 July |
Sydney 08:57 6 July

Sensitive, caring Cancer is ruled by the moon, making this new moon the ideal time to really tune in to how we feel about life, love and the universe. Intentions focused on our homes and family life make sense when the moon is in Cancer, making now a great time to plan for the future.

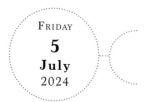

NEW MOON INTENTIONS FOR YOUR SIGN

Let your intuition guide you this new moon

ARIES	♈	Make a commitment that puts your family life first.
TAURUS	♉	Be brave enough to tell someone a few home truths.
GEMINI	♊	Get clear on what's important to you and make it a priority.
CANCER	♋	Trust your intuition on an important next step in your life.
LEO	♌	Leave the past in the past once and for all.
VIRGO	♍	Join a community, club or group and stand up for a cause.
LIBRA	♎	Set a career goal that can offer the work-life balance you need.
SCORPIO	♏	Make a travel plan with a close friend or family member you need quality time with.
SAGITTARIUS	♐	Face up to a difficult truth that's holding you back.
CAPRICORN	♑	If you're ready to commit, make it happen.
AQUARIUS	♒	Find a new and inspiring way to start your day.
PISCES	♓	Step into the spotlight and enjoy your success.

Sunday
21
July
2024

FULL MOON IN CAPRICORN

London 11:17 | New York 06:17 | Los Angeles 03:17 | Tokyo 19:17 | Sydney 20:17

The full Buck Moon falls in ambitious Capricorn for a second consecutive month bringing serious double-down vibes to anything that went on this time last month. If you've been hanging out for a second chance to do away with self-sabotage and step into your power, July's full moon is the one. It's time to believe in miracles.

FULL MOON THEMES & QUESTIONS FOR YOUR SIGN

	THEMES	ASK YOURSELF
ARIES ♈	Refining a career goal, making a move forwards, trying again, feeling increasingly positive about an ambitious dream for the future	*What is holding me back from achieving my goals?*
TAURUS ♉	Losing yourself in a subject, saying 'Yes' to spontaneous plans, booking flights or tickets, being more sure of an escape plan than ever before	*When do I feel the most free?*
GEMINI ♊	Turning a passion project into a business idea, discovering a secret that changes your thinking, facing your demons, life-changing financial news	*What matters most to me now?*
CANCER ♋	Pushing forwards with a plan to team up with someone else in life or love, making a big gesture you failed to make last month, finding love somewhere unexpected	*What is stopping me from following my heart?*

Attune to the magic of the Capricorn full moon

		THEMES	ASK YOURSELF
LEO	♌	Doubling down on a health kick, seeing results, feeling good, pledging to stick at it for good	*What can I add to my life to make it even better?*
VIRGO	♍	Allowing yourself to step into the spotlight, feeling love from afar, a big creative success, discovering a new hobby you adore	*What truly lights me up?*
LIBRA	♎	Making a serious commitment, changing your home or family set-up, finding a solid foundation, feeling ready to settle down	*Why did I resist this for so long?*
SCORPIO	♏	Sharing your story with a wide audience, telling it like it is, learning something new, connecting with others	*How can I build upon the connections I've made?*
SAGITTARIUS	♐	Seeing an investment pay off, trusting your instincts, knowing you're worth it, making sure someone else knows that too	*Why can't I ask for more?*
CAPRICORN	♑	Reinventing yourself, building your own dream instead of someone else's, making plans for the future, aiming high	*How can I think even bigger?*
AQUARIUS	♒	Following a spiritual path, making time for yoga or other practices, feeling stronger, leaving the past where it belongs	*How can I take the first step into my future?*
PISCES	♓	Amassing a following on or offline, people listening to what you have to say, throwing an event or party, learning to lead	*What is my biggest goal right now?*

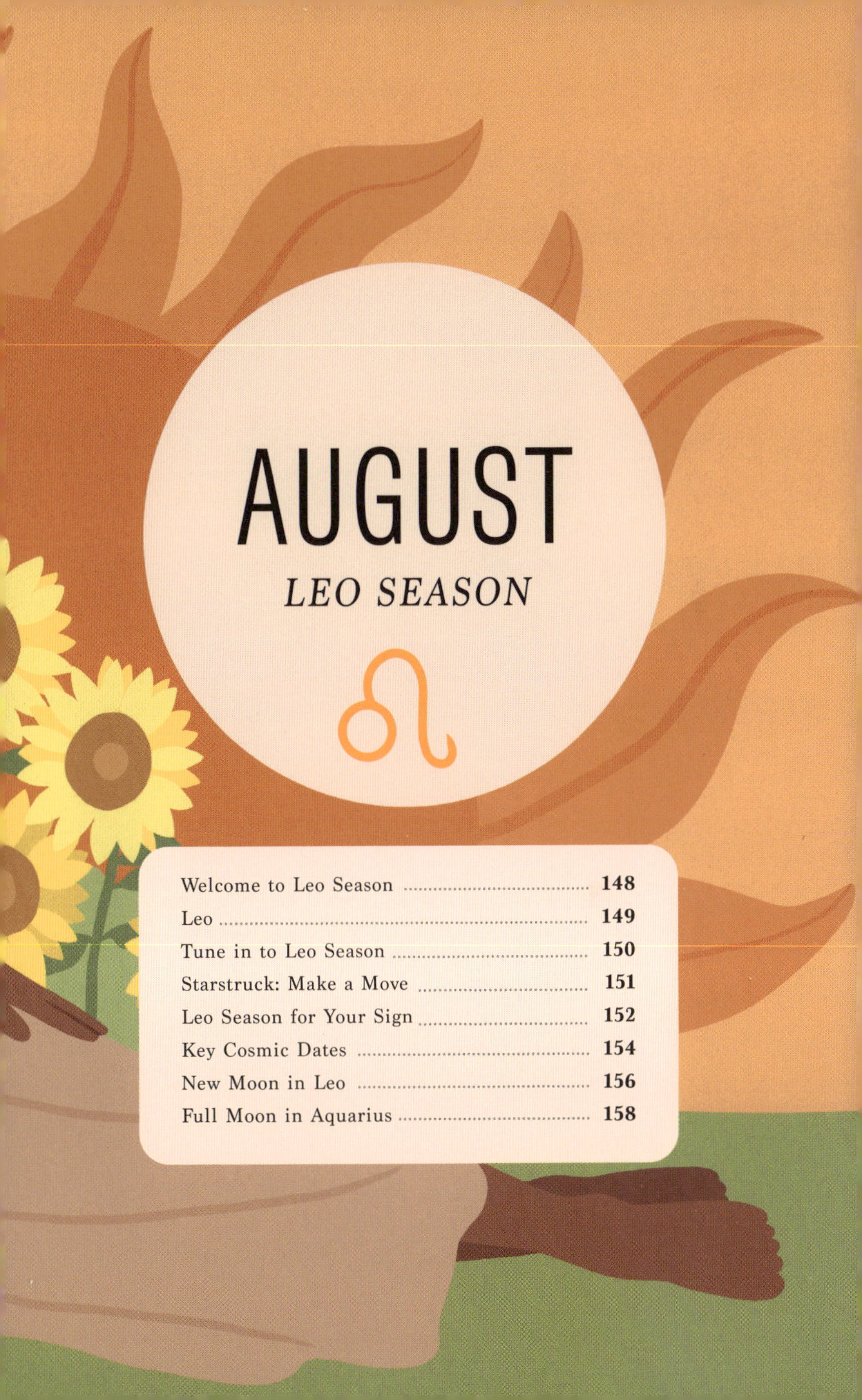

AUGUST

LEO SEASON

♌

Welcome to Leo Season 148

Leo 149

Tune in to Leo Season 150

Starstruck: Make a Move 151

Leo Season for Your Sign 152

Key Cosmic Dates 154

New Moon in Leo 156

Full Moon in Aquarius 158

WELCOME TO LEO SEASON

Grab your darkest sunglasses because Leo is ready to shine. The zodiac's ultimate main character brings life, soul and superstar vibes to the party as summer hits its peak. Happiest in the middle of the action - and ideally centre of attention - Leo is a sign that's impossible to ignore and easy to love. Gregarious, big-hearted and ruled by the sun, this sign was born to dazzle.

It's easy to know where you stand with Leo because they wear their hearts on their sleeves. If you're important to them, they'll make sure you know it by showering you with love, gifts and affection. And their protective loyalty knows no bounds. Those good vibes won't last long if you don't reciprocate, though. Leo is generous to a fault but above all else they want to be seen, witnessed and adored. Make sure Leo knows quite how wonderful you think they are and they'll be on your side forever.

It doesn't take much for Leo's larger-than-life approach to tip over into me-me-me territory. This is a sign with big feelings, big ideas and zero tolerance for delayed gratification. Leo wants it all and wants it now - and if that means throwing a hissy fit to get to the front of the queue so be it. To tame this sign's wild side would be to temper some of their best qualities - passion, confidence, flamboyance - but a few soothing words can go a long way towards smoothing ruffled manes.

There's a childlike quality to Leo that's magical to be around - they're brilliantly creative and know how to make a good time out of any situation. Appearances matter to this expressive sign so expect them to be overdressed - and ready for their close up - at all times. Leo brings the drama, Leo fuels the drama, Leo is the drama - life is never boring with a lion in tow.

LEO

22 July–21 August

THE MAIN CHARACTER - *Gregarious. Dramatic. Generous. Protective.*

SYMBOL	Lion
RULED BY	Sun
ELEMENT	Fire
MODALITY	Fixed
RULES THE	5th House of Fun, Creativity, Romance & Children
LUCKY DAY	Sunday
STAR STONE	Tiger's Eye
SOUL FLOWER	Sunflower
AT THEIR BEST	Big-hearted, loyal, passionate, entertaining
AT THEIR WORST	Pushy, excessive, egotistical, self-obsessed
TAROT CARD	Strength

LEO 101

VIBE	Fun-loving party animal who loves the spotlight
STYLE	Bodycon, bold brights, animal print, full-on glamour, edgy designers, statement everything
LOVES	Being the centre of attention
HATES	Parties having to end
MOST LIKELY TO	Rule the world
JUST DON'T	Ever ignore them
FIND THEM	At the end of a queue of admirers, winning at life, making an entrance, paying the bill, performing on stage, going live on Instagram
BORN TO	Shine

TUNE IN TO LEO SEASON

Shine bright this August

BE BRAVE Use the energy of Leo season to push yourself out of your comfort zone and go for gold. It's time to feel the fear and do it anyway.

EXPRESS YOURSELF Write, paint, cook, craft, dance, act, sculpt – carving out time for anything that sets your creative side free is the ideal Leo season activity.

LOVE HARD Love is all Leo needs so take a few tips from the lionheart this August. Tell someone how you feel about them. Show your appreciation. Send spontaneous gifts. Or flowers. Or fly them to Paris for a dramatic proposal.

BE A BIT MUCH Leo is never afraid to be a bit much – and that's why we love them! Allow yourself the freedom to let it all out this August. Speak the truth, cry the tears, shout from the rooftops and do it all wearing sequins.

EMBRACE YOUR INNER CHILD Remember what lit you up when you were younger and find a way to fit more of that into your life now. Rediscovering a love of fashion, team sports, reading or art is a very Leo vibe.

GET LOUD Tap into some Leo season energy and show the world what you're made of. Now is not the time for playing small. Announce your arrival. Launch the business. Be the star. And tell it like it is.

STARSTRUCK

MAKE A MOVE

Leo season can feel a bit much at times. The sun! The FOMO! The beach body pressure! Reclaim your power this summer by embracing movement for movement's sake – for fun, for freedom, for the hell of it. If the suggestions below don't work for you and your body, Leo season is also a great time to seek out some sunshine, get creative or just do more of whatever makes you happy.

FEEL BETTER THAN EVER THIS SUMMER

ARIES	♈	Fiery Aries thrives on competition so try CrossFit, Peloton or anything with a leaderboard you can smash.
TAURUS	♉	Long walks in nature are the perfect salve for slow and steady Taurus.
GEMINI	♊	Team sports are a winner for easily bored Gemini.
CANCER	♋	An online yoga or Pilates session from the living room works perfectly for homebody Cancer.
LEO	♌	A celeb-endorsed spin class at the hottest studio in town should be enough to get Leo moving.
VIRGO	♍	Solo outdoor pursuits such as paddleboarding and kayaking work well for earthy Virgo.
LIBRA	♎	It's all about grace and beauty for peace-seeking Libra so try ballet, barre or modern dance.
SCORPIO	♏	Hot yoga, boxing and anything involving a dimly lit underground gym.
SAGITTARIUS	♐	Movement and adventure go hand in hand for Sagittarius. Think waterskiing, snowboarding or white-water rafting.
CAPRICORN	♑	Ambitious Capricorn likes to see results. Weight training, running or rock-climbing all have what it takes.
AQUARIUS	♒	As long as it doesn't involving repetitive moves at the gym, Aquarius is all in. Trampolining, TRX sessions or skateboarding could be just the ticket.
PISCES	♓	If it involves water Pisces is on board. Wild swimming and surfing are where the magic happens.

LEO SEASON FOR YOUR SIGN

♈ ARIES Let the good times roll, Aries. What you need most right now is fun and that's exactly what's on the cards if the cosmos gets its way this month.

If you do one thing this month: Go out more.

♉ TAURUS It's time to put yourself at the top of the priority list, Taurus. Treat yourself as you treat others and you'll go far this month.

If you do one thing this month: Up the self-care.

♊ GEMINI A big idea that hits when you least expect it could change your world this month. Pay attention to that gut feeling.

If you do one thing this month: Reconnect with a sibling or close friend.

♋ CANCER Allow envy to become inspiration this month as you work towards a big goal. Your financial future may depend on your next move.

If you do one thing this month: Treat yourself.

♌ LEO It's show time! Bring on the birthday glitz and make like the star you know you are. There's magic in celebrating just how far you've come.

If you do one thing this month: Throw a party.

♍ VIRGO A summer break that prioritizes your wellbeing is exactly what you need. Think yoga and sea swims not rosé and partying and you'll be on the right track.

If you do one thing this month: Explore your spiritual side.

♎ **LIBRA** Standing up for what you believe in could lead to a magical new connection this month. Believe in karma – you will reap what you sow.

If you do one thing this month: RSVP 'Yes'.

♏ **SCORPIO** How do you want to be remembered, Scorpio? This month could offer an opportunity to take a step in the right direction.

If you do one thing this month: Expect more.

♐ **SAGITTARIUS** Need for a break from the same-old, same-old? Choose adventure, travel or new beginnings this month and enjoy your great escape.

If you do one thing this month: Find your muse.

♑ **CAPRICORN** A deep connection that comes out of nowhere could rock your world this Leo season. Think before you act too impulsively on this one.

If you do one thing this month: Be open to change.

♒ **AQUARIUS** A partnership with the potential to change your world could mean making a big commitment this month. Are you ready to go for it?

If you do one thing this month: Team up.

♓ **PISCES** Try not to let your summer plans sabotage your wellbeing. Stay focused on a goal that makes your life better and end Leo season happier than ever.

If you do one thing this month: Don't quit.

AUGUST

Key Cosmic Dates

LUGHNASADH
1 August
A celebration that marks the beginning of the harvest and is halfway between the summer solstice and autumn equinox.

NEW MOON LEO
4 August
It's good vibes all round with a new moon in sunny Leo. Share the love, find the magic and enjoy the ride.

MERCURY RETROGRADE BEGINS
5 August
Turn interruptions into opportunities to slow down and you'll soon see the magic behind the mayhem (see p93 and p124).

VENUS ENTERS VIRGO
5 August
Love doesn't have to be perfect but when Venus is in Virgo it's going to give it a damned good try.

MERCURY RETROGRADE LEAVES VIRGO
15 August
The planet's backspin moves from perfectionist Virgo to creative Leo – time to revisit a stalled project or forgotten dream.

FULL MOON IN AQUARIUS
19 August
The power of this moon lies in standing up for others and gathering together to create lasting change.

VIRGO SEASON BEGINS
22 August
Summer isn't over yet but Virgo season knows now is the time to start shaping up for September.

MERCURY RETROGRADE ENDS
28 August
Big sighs of relief as life gets back on track in time for back-to-school season.

VENUS ENTERS LIBRA
29 August
Creating harmony in our relationships becomes a focus when this planet takes a spin through Libra.

RETROGRADE (RX) PLANETS

PLUTO RX
2 May–12 October
(2 May–2 September
in Aquarius;
2 September–12 Oct
in Capricorn)

SATURN RX
29 June–
15 November
in Pisces

NEPTUNE RX
2 July–7 December
in Pisces

MERCURY RX
5–28 August
(5–15 in Virgo;
15–28 in Leo)

SUNDAY
4
August
2024

NEW MOON IN LEO

London 12:13 | New York 07:13 | Los Angeles 04:13 | Tokyo 20:13 | Sydney 21:13

A new moon in expressive, big-hearted Leo is the perfect time to recommit to living life to the fullest. Leo energy is bold, creative and unafraid to stand out from the crowd, making this the ideal time to step into the spotlight and show the world what you're really made of.

NEW MOON INTENTIONS FOR YOUR SIGN

Make a brave move this new moon

ARIES	♈	Get comfortable in your own skin and become who you really are.
TAURUS	♉	Take steps towards making a relocation or holiday home plan your reality.
GEMINI	♊	Lay your cards on the table this summer.
CANCER	♋	Refuse to settle for second best in life or love.
LEO	♌	Make a big move towards the future you dream about.
VIRGO	♍	Forgive, forget and move on with your life.
LIBRA	♎	Celebrate the friends and family you know always have your back.
SCORPIO	♏	Take a passion project on the road with you this month.
SAGITTARIUS	♐	Sign up for an adventure or challenge that scares you.
CAPRICORN	♑	Trust that big changes in your life are meant to be.
AQUARIUS	♒	Take the romantic hint and make a move.
PISCES	♓	Recommit to a wellbeing practice that changed your life earlier this year.

Monday
19
August
2024

FULL MOON IN AQUARIUS

London 19:26 | New York 14:26 | Los Angeles 11:26 | Tokyo 03:26 20 August | Sydney 04:26 20 August

A full moon in humanitarian Aquarius asks us to be the change we want to see in the world. The friendships and communities we care about fall into focus under this moon but there's no place for social one-upmanship with the Sturgeon Moon. It urges us to let go of old ideas about who we are and what we're worth and join together to stand up for what we believe in. It is also a seasonal Blue Moon, which means it's the third full moon in a season with four.

FULL MOON THEMES & QUESTIONS FOR YOUR SIGN

	THEMES	ASK YOURSELF
ARIES ♈	Supporting a cause, gathering people together, making new friends, feeling part of something important	*Who do I need to surround myself with now?*
TAURUS ♉	Quitting the day job, going it alone at work, creating a change in office culture, disrupting your industry	*Who says it has to be this way?*
GEMINI ♊	Finding something to believe in, working to live instead of living to work, making major travel plans, finding new solutions to old problems	*How can I take my life to the next level?*
CANCER ♋	Finding financial support for a project, undergoing a personal transformation, learning to cope with a difficult time in your life, focusing in on a new goal or passion	*How can I give myself a break?*

Attune to the magic of the Aquarius full moon

	THEMES	ASK YOURSELF
LEO ♌	Making a commitment to someone, teaming up for a project, finding love, accepting the help you need, creating something beautiful	*Can I find a way to give more than I take?*
VIRGO ♍	Changing your daily routine, turning anger into action, putting your health first, taking the first steps towards a big goal	*What am I ready to change this summer?*
LIBRA ♎	Throwing a party to celebrate an achievement, finding a creative solution, feeling happier than you have in a long time, prioritizing joy in your life	*What parts of myself am I no longer willing to hide?*
SCORPIO ♏	Spending time with friends who feel like family, switching up your living situation, finding a community, feeling more secure in your choices, stepping away from the past and into your future	*What do I need to let go of to move forwards?*
SAGITTARIUS ♐	Finding someone you can really talk to, sharing your story to help others, taking on a writing project, getting into journalling, learning something new	*How can I express myself more clearly?*
CAPRICORN ♑	Feeling stronger than ever, knowing your own power, gathering resources, putting yourself first, watching your bank balance skyrocket	*What investment do I need to make now?*
AQUARIUS ♒	Starting a new adventure, standing up for what's right, becoming who you really are, embracing your individuality, finding your people, feeling free	*Why am I afraid to be myself with some people?*
PISCES ♓	Knowing your limits, asking for help, committing to a spiritual practice, spending time alone, taking a break, finding inner peace	*How can I clear my diary so I can totally relax?*

SEPTEMBER

VIRGO SEASON

♍

Welcome to Virgo Season 162
Virgo 163
Tune in to Virgo Season 164
Starstruck: Autumn Equinox 165
Virgo Season for Your Sign 166
Key Cosmic Dates 168
New Moon in Virgo 170
Full Moon Eclipse in Pisces 172

WELCOME TO VIRGO SEASON

If you want a job doing properly, get a Virgo on the case. A walking, talking back-to-school vibe, this perfectionist earth sign gets its kicks from routine, organization and next-level productivity. There's no showy drama with Virgo in charge, just hard graft, high standards and satisfying ticks off the To Do list. In fact, the only thing Virgo loves more than a plan is making that plan come together, one considered move at a time. The zodiac's quiet achiever doesn't shout their success from the rooftops because they don't need external validation - Virgo knows that the sky is the limit, one step at a time.

It's important not to write Virgo off as critical, picky or uptight, too. Under the wrong circumstances they can be all those things but at the heart of the matter, Virgo just wants what's best for themselves and those they care about. Virgo is nothing if not discerning! If Virgo chooses you for their team - in life, love or business - you're on to a winner. This is a sign that selects its allegiances with care, attention and a subconscious checklist. If you're in, you're in, and that's definitely something to celebrate.

The side of Virgo you'll get to know once you've made the inner circle is nothing short of magical. Pay close attention and you'll soon notice this sign is happiest stirring something up in the kitchen, practising yoga at sunrise or worshipping the elements in the great outdoors. Virgos are natural earth mothers, instinctive healers, creative alchemists, witches and magic makers. They're hard on themselves because they want to get it right, they're easily stressed because they try so hard, they lack flexibility because they want to stay in control, but they hold life-changing power in the palms of their hands.

Inspiration is never in short supply with Virgo on the scene. This is a sign on a mission to make life as wonderful as it possibly can be. A sign that knows health really is wealth. A sign that believes the journey matters just as much as the destination. A sign that always wants to do better, not for money or acclaim, but because they care. A sign that should really give themselves a break because they're already enough just as they are.

VIRGO

22 August–21 September

THE HEALER - *Health-conscious. Productive. Analytical. Discerning.*

SYMBOL	Maiden
RULED BY	Mercury
ELEMENT	Earth
MODALITY	Mutable
RULES THE	6th House of Daily Routines, Health & Hard Work
LUCKY DAY	Wednesday
STAR STONE	Lapis lazuli
SOUL FLOWER	Daisy
AT THEIR BEST	Helpful, hard-working, inspiring, selfless
AT THEIR WORST	Critical, picky, perfectionist, stressed out
TAROT CARD	The Hermit

VIRGO 101

VIBE	Inspiring, health-conscious grafter who's happiest outdoors
STYLE	Clean lines, shiny shoes, winter white, yoga pants, Dryrobes, capsule wardrobes, athleisure
LOVES	A sunrise
HATES	Procrastination
MOST LIKELY TO	Arrive early
JUST DON'T	Mess with their schedule
FIND THEM	Colour-coding their bookshelves, working out, ticking off To Dos, winning at life, necking green smoothies, helping others, cleaning up the mess you can't see, setting a 6am alarm at the weekend
BORN TO	Be employee of the month

TUNE IN TO VIRGO SEASON

Bring on the back-to-school vibes

CREATE A MORNING ROUTINE Virgo knows that the way you start the day shapes the rest of it, so why not make it more magical? Create a routine that celebrates you and your priorities whether that means 6am yoga and green smoothies or journalling over tea in bed.

GET ORGANIZED Channel Virgo's ability to nail a To Do list by finding ways to make life run more smoothly this month. Invest in a new diary, start filing your receipts, order a recipe box delivery, tidy your desk, hire a cleaner... whatever it takes.

BE MORE DISCERNING Virgo's perfectionist side is more about discernment than it is about pickiness. Why settle for less when you could reach for the stars? Try applying a little discernment of your own when deciding what and who to prioritize this month.

PUT IN THE WORK You can have amazing ideas and endless big dreams but nothing will happen if you don't put the graft in. Embrace some of Virgo's 'get it done' spirit and start something you've been putting off.

GET HEALTH CONSCIOUS Virgo urges all of us to leave the excesses of summer behind as September hits its stride. Think about what you can add to your life rather than what you can cut out... more fruit, more vegetables, more sleep, more enjoyable ways to move your body.

STARSTRUCK

AUTUMN EQUINOX

22 September

The autumn equinox is a celebration of abundance as day and night balance out on the path to hibernation season. Traditionally associated with harvest, it's the perfect time to reflect on the year so far and practise gratitude as summer shuts up shop. This is a season for stillness, planning and taking stock.

CELEBRATE THE AUTUMN EQUINOX

Ways to reflect, respect and mark this turn of the wheel

HOST A FEAST

Embrace the colours and flavours of the season to come with aromatic spices, roasted pumpkin, salted caramel and toasted marshmallows. Host a last barbecue, organize a pot-luck supper or create the ultimate grazing platter.

LIGHT UP YOUR LIFE

Stoke up the firepit, make a bonfire or light every candle you own for some equinox reflection and intention setting.

GET A GOAL BACK ON TRACK

The autumn equinox might symbolize the beginning of the darker, quieter half of the year but with over three months left of 2024, it's also a great time to revisit your goals. What do you want to achieve or do before the year is out?

PRACTISE GRATITUDE

Write a list of everything you're grateful for in your life as the sun sets or rises on the autumn equinox.

REFLECT AND BE STILL

We can learn a lot from nature as it begins to slowly prepare for the winter months ahead – gathering, nesting, retreating and resting are as important as celebrating abundance during the autumn equinox.

VIRGO SEASON FOR YOUR SIGN

♈ ARIES It's shake it off and shake it up time, Aries. Switch up your morning routine, recommit to a task that needs ticking off your list and put your health first.

If you do one thing this month: Put in the work.

♉ TAURUS Be brave enough to step out of your comfort zone and into the spotlight and you won't believe the magic that follows. Creative success awaits!

If you do one thing this month: Do more of what makes you happy.

♊ GEMINI House moves and family news could both feature this month. Know that life doesn't have to happen in the right order to be exactly as it is meant to be.

If you do one thing this month: Take the leap.

♋ CANCER A heart-to-heart you've been putting off for fear of the outcome can't wait a moment longer. It might even evolve into a dream come true.

If you do one thing this month: Speak from the heart.

♌ LEO An investment you made earlier this year could begin to pay off in the most incredible way this month. And if that investment was one you made in yourself, keep going!

If you do one thing this month: Believe in yourself.

♍ VIRGO It's birthday season and time for another Virgo reinvention. How do you want to live now? Who do you want to be? You've totally got this.

If you do one thing this month: Make the change.

♎ LIBRA If you're brave enough to face up to an uncomfortable truth this month you'll soon be on a new path forwards. Forgive yourself.

If you do one thing this month: Heal your heart.

♏ SCORPIO New connections, new challenges and new possibilities make September ripe with potential. Pay attention to who you're with when you feel your best, Scorpio.

If you do one thing this month: Follow up on an offer or introduction.

♐ SAGITTARIUS Renewed enthusiasm for a passion project or career goal could see you working harder than ever this month. Know the rewards will be worth it.

If you do one thing this month: Set a new goal.

♑ CAPRICORN Embarking on a course of study or private exploration of a subject that fascinates you could spell the beginning of something magical this month.

If you do one thing this month: Follow your interests.

♒ AQUARIUS Someone with the power to change your financial future could make an offer you can't refuse this month. What's stopping you?

If you do one thing this month: Go for it.

♓ PISCES You're in a better place than you realize when it comes to love and relationships, Pisces. Look around you! You made this happen for all the right reasons.

If you do one thing this month: Feel the love.

SEPTEMBER

Key Cosmic Dates

URANUS RETROGRADE BEGINS *1 September*	Personal breakthroughts and intense self-reflection could feature this retrograde.
NEW MOON IN VIRGO *3 September*	The fresh start we all need. This is the ideal time to set intentions and make changes.
MARS ENTERS CANCER *4 September*	Feelings can get intense with passionate Mars in emotional Cancer. Allow yourself to feel it all but avoid wallowing to excess.
MERCURY ENTERS VIRGO *9 September*	An extra kick of get-it-done energy arrives. Use it to tick off To Dos like never before.
FULL MOON ECLIPSE IN PISCES *18 September*	A full super moon lunar eclipse in mystical Pisces offers powerful insight into our biggest and bravest dreams.
LIBRA SEASON BEGINS *22 September*	Peace, love and great outfits rule when the sun is in Libra. Find and feel the love and celebrate the beauty that surrounds you.
AUTUMN EQUINOX *22 September*	Day and night become equal once more. A great time for gratitude and reflection
VENUS ENTERS SCORPIO *23 September*	Things can get seriously steamy with love planet Venus in mysterious Scorpio. Fall in lust, blow caution to the wind and leap before you look – just take care of your heart.

RETROGRADE (RX) PLANETS

PLUTO RX
2 May–12 October
(2 May–2 September
in Aquarius;
2 September–12 October
in Capricorn)

SATURN RX
29 June–
15 November
in Pisces

NEPTUNE RX
2 July–7 December
in Pisces

URANUS RX
1 September–
30 January 2025
in Taurus

TUESDAY
3
September
2024

NEW MOON IN VIRGO

London 02:55 | New York 21:55 2 September | Los Angeles 18:55 2 September | Tokyo 10:55 | Sydney 11:55

A new moon in practical, hard-working, health-conscious Virgo is the cosmic reset we all need as September begins. Now is the time to decide what you want to make happen in the final part of 2024 and set an intention to go get it. New routines, healthy living and hard work that pays off all look lit under this new moon.

NEW MOON INTENTIONS FOR YOUR SIGN

Do what needs doing and expect results

ARIES	♈	Get organized, get healthy and activate a plan.
TAURUS	♉	Share a passion project with the world.
GEMINI	♊	Start a project that takes you closer to home.
CANCER	♋	Tell someone how you really feel.
LEO	♌	Work hard now for a lucrative future.
VIRGO	♍	Work towards your biggest goal and know it'll be worth it.
LIBRA	♎	Forgive someone to set yourself free.
SCORPIO	♏	Reach out to someone with the power to change your life.
SAGITTARIUS	♐	Take a big leap towards your greatest-ever success.
CAPRICORN	♑	Commit to learning more about something that enriches your life.
AQUARIUS	♒	Find your focus and go for it.
PISCES	♓	Shape up your life to show someone you care.

♍ SEPTEMBER

Wednesday 18 September 2024

FULL MOON ECLIPSE IN PISCES

London 03:34 | New York 22:34
17 September | Los Angeles 19:34
17 September | Tokyo 11:34 | Sydney 12:34

Expect a big reveal as the full super Corn Moon eclipse in Pisces brings themes of closure, healing and dreams. Watch and wait is always a good tactic during an eclipse and this full super moon, also known as the Harvest Moon, is no exception. Pay attention to what comes up for you during this lunation – signs, dreams, sudden realizations about life, the universe and everything – and allow it all to wash over you. The magic of a full moon eclipse is often in what comes next.

FULL MOON THEMES & QUESTIONS FOR YOUR SIGN

	THEMES	ASK YOURSELF
ARIES ♈	Discovering an important truth, finding power in your own intuition, feeling ready to move on from your past	*Could forgiving someone help me move on?*
TAURUS ♉	Realizing where you fit in with a group of friends or colleagues, wanting to find your people, knowing who you want to spend more time with	*When do I feel most free to be myself?*
GEMINI ♊	Dreaming bigger than ever, understanding what your next big goal is, working out what it is you need to do to get there	*Who says my wildest dreams can't come true?*
CANCER ♋	Feeling at home somewhere new, wanting to explore, learning new things, being honest with yourself and others, dreaming of travel	*How can I make my life feel bigger?*

Attune to the magic of the Pisces full moon eclipse

	THEMES	ASK YOURSELF
LEO ♌	Discovering a secret, facing the truth, falling in lust, ignoring the rules, playing with fire, becoming obsessed with something or someone	*Do I need a reality check right now?*
VIRGO ♍	Becoming a better partner (in love, work or friendship), changing priorities, making connections, making big plans with someone you love	*Am I as committed as they seem to think I am?*
LIBRA ♎	Putting your health first, asking for help, working on yourself, releasing an old habit or way of doing things, changing your ways	*What will be different this time?*
SCORPIO ♏	Feeling flirtatious, planning a celebration, spending time with children or young people, getting creative, feeling grateful	*What do I need to let go of to move forwards?*
SAGITTARIUS ♐	Realizing who you can count on, creating your own version of family, feeling overwhelmed, moving house, investing in the future, spending time with a mother figure	*Why can't I enjoy life?*
CAPRICORN ♑	Sharing a story that makes a difference, speaking up for someone who needs you, writing or speaking about your life or work, talking something through, finding your power	*How can I look after myself better?*
AQUARIUS ♒	Increasing your bank balance, signing a big deal, accepting a pay rise, feeling valued, investing in yourself or others, feeling free	*How can I turn my talents into gold?*
PISCES ♓	Starting over, quitting the self-sabotage, knowing your worth, letting yourself be known, feeling strong, changing your life	*What will help me embrace my success?*

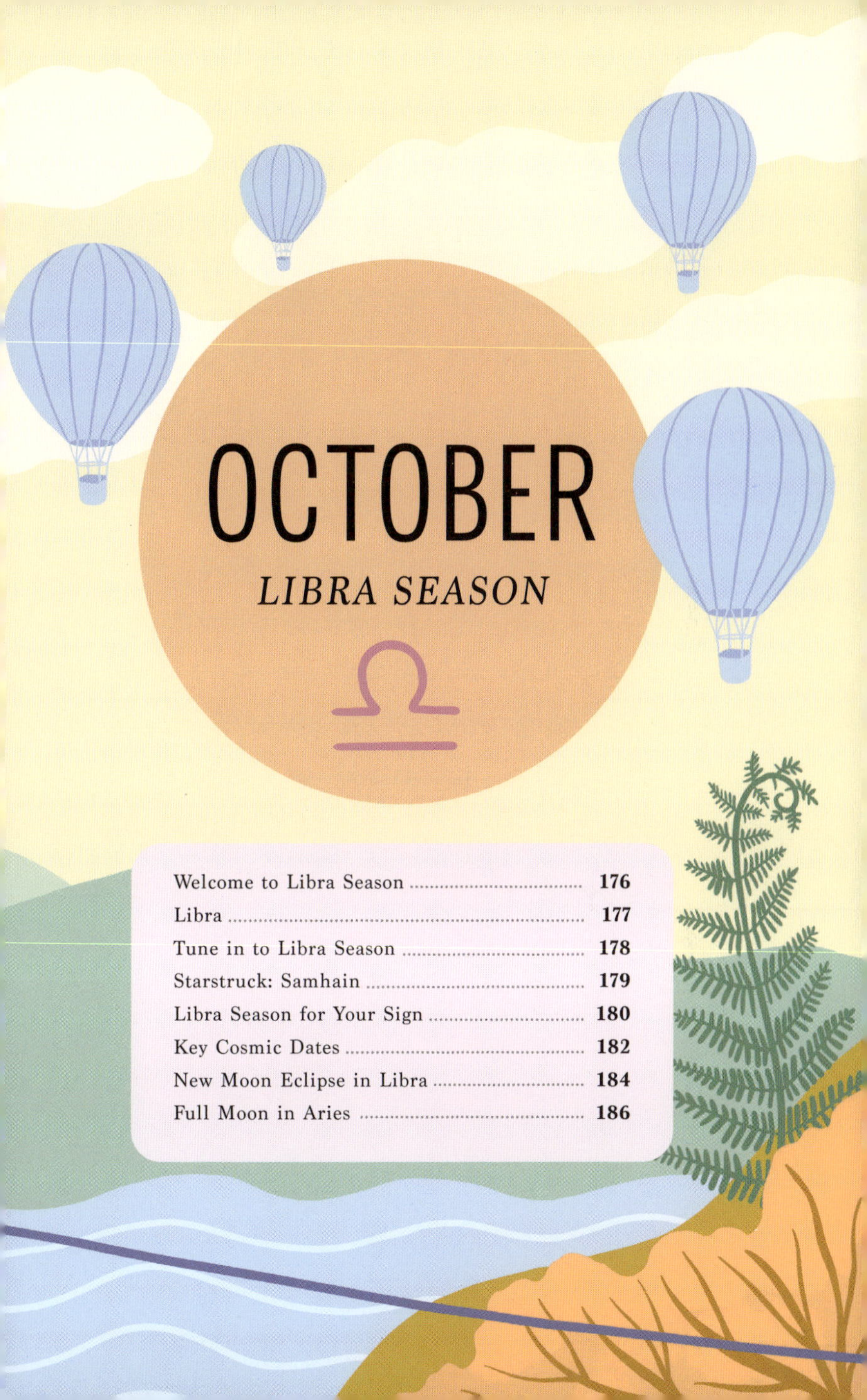

OCTOBER

LIBRA SEASON

♎

Welcome to Libra Season 176
Libra 177
Tune in to Libra Season 178
Starstruck: Samhain 179
Libra Season for Your Sign 180
Key Cosmic Dates 182
New Moon Eclipse in Libra 184
Full Moon in Aries 186

WELCOME TO LIBRA SEASON

If you don't already have a Libra in your life, you might want to try and get one. Stylish, charming and easy-going, spend even a short amount of time with this social air sign and you'll understand why everyone wants in on the action. Libra is happiest when the people around them are happy, which makes them perfect hosts, agreeable companions and pleasingly cooperative colleagues. Libra wants nothing more than to be liked by everyone who crosses their path – and therein lies a problem.

Relationships matter a great deal to this enchanting sign. Libra loves love, hates confrontation and can't bear to cause offence. Libra finds it easy to win people over, make connections and understand both sides of the story. Libra is loyal, committed and quick to compromise. Libra invests so much energy into pleasing other people they have very little left for themselves. And don't even think about asking them to make a decision.

Untangling their thoughts, feelings and opinions from those of the people they care about can be a lifelong challenge for this obliging sign. Diplomatic to the core, it takes a great deal of time, energy and gentle probing to persuade Libra to choose a side, speak their mind or find a bad word to say about anyone. Live life with Libra and you'll soon know that what sounds sweet and caring can easily tip into frustrating territory when they just won't tell you what they want.

Libra might be a social chameleon but they always stand out in a crowd. Aesthetics matter as much as relationships to idealistic Librans, which means their homes, Instagram feeds and party looks are all styled to perfection. Compliment them on the above and they'll love you forever.

Harmony, balance and inner peace are all important to this sign but that doesn't mean they don't have a wild side. Find the party and you'll find Libra holding court, flirting with strangers and making everyone feel like they're the most important person they've ever been lucky enough to meet.

LIBRA

22 September–21 October

THE PEACE-SEEKER - *Stylish. Loveable. Enchanting. Balanced.*

SYMBOL	Scales
RULED BY	Venus
ELEMENT	Air
MODALITY	Cardinal
RULES THE	7th House of Love, Romance, Relationships & Duos
LUCKY DAY	Friday
STAR STONE	Opal
SOUL FLOWER	Hydrangea
AT THEIR BEST	Charming, accommodating, adorable, social
AT THEIR WORST	People pleaser, indecisive, superficial, overthinker
TAROT CARD	Justice

LIBRA 101

VIBE	Stylish, artistic peacemaker who knows how to work a room
STYLE	Luxe loungewear, red carpet glamour, pristine cashmere, chic separates, swanky lingerie, looking the part
LOVES	A makeover
HATES	Bad vibes
MOST LIKELY TO	Charm their way to the top
JUST DON'T	Ever ask them to choose sides
FIND THEM	Falling in love, wandering art galleries, writing thank-you notes, working the room, fending off admirers, swerving an argument, styling their interiors, photographing their lunch
BORN TO	Be adored

TUNE IN TO LIBRA SEASON

Peace out this October

FALL IN LOVE If there's one thing Libra loves it's love itself – good news for anyone hoping to bring more romance into their life. Max out on Libra season vibes by showing someone you care, taking a relationship to the next level or getting back on the apps.

TURN ON THE CHARM Libra knows that a little charm goes a long way so try turning yours up a notch this month. Smile at strangers, ask nicely and don't be afraid to flirt to get what you want.

PUT SOMEONE ELSE FIRST Libra might take this to extremes at times but we can all learn something from this sign's ability to give more than they take. Not sure you've got it in you? Then it's even more important that you try.

BEAUTIFY YOUR WORLD Start the renovation project, style up your space, invest in art, rebrand your social media or showcase a hot new look on your commute. There's no shame in prioritizing aesthetics in Libra season.

HAVE IT BOTH WAYS Spend any amount of time with Libra and you'll soon understand that indecision comes with the territory. But does life really have to be binary? Listen to alternative views, try the other option, give both ways a go... sometimes there's magic in refusing to choose.

GET OUT THERE People pleaser or people person, it's all the same to Libra as long as there's good conversation, meaningful connection and someone to admire their outfit. Get out there and socialize while the going is good.

STARSTRUCK

SAMHAIN

31 October

There's magic in the air as the wheel of the year (see p23) turns to usher in the ancient fire festival of Samhain, thought of by some as New Year for witches. Many of the traditions we associate with Halloween originate from the Celtic spiritual traditions associated with this festival, a time of encroaching darkness, final harvest and connection with the spirit world.

CELEBRATE SAMHAIN

Make some magic while the veil is thin

MAKE AN ALTAR

Create an altar celebrating the past, present and future at this time of seasonal transition. Add candles, art, oracle cards, flowers, crystal skulls, carved pumpkins, incense, ancestor offerings and pictures of the people who have helped you become who you are today.

HOST A DUMB SUPPER

A dumb - or silent - supper involves making a beautiful meal and setting extra places at the table for ancestors no longer with us. It's a magical way to remember, celebrate and connect to those we have loved and lost while the veil between the worlds is thin.

REFLECT AND RENEW

Many modern witches consider Samhain their New Year, making it a great time for quiet reflection and contemplation. Swerve the Halloween chaos and spend some time thinking, relaxing and journalling about what's next for you.

CAST A SPELL

Make the most of the Samhain magic by casting a spell. Light candles in a colour connected to something you wish to call in to your life (red for passion, green for prosperity, yellow for creativity) and make a magical wish.

DRESS UP

Go ghoulish if you want but there's also magic in bringing style and glamour to the fashion table at Samhain. Whether you're in solo contemplation or celebrating with friends and family, take the time to dress up and embody the person you wish to be in the months to come.

LIBRA SEASON FOR YOUR SIGN

♈ ARIES It's time to switch things up in a relationship that matters. All take and no give isn't working for you (or them) this time.

If you do one thing this month: Make time for love.

♉ TAURUS No more excuses, Taurus! There's a job that needs doing and you're the one to do it. Let 'start now, finish sooner' be your motto this month.

If you do one thing this month: Make a plan.

♊ GEMINI If you've been waiting all year for someone to notice you, your luck is in. Not sure how to deal with what happens next? Listen to your heart.

If you do one thing this month: Allow yourself to be adored.

♋ CANCER Put your own needs to the top of the priority list this Libra season and you might avoid a crash further down the line. Is it time you learnt how to mother yourself?

If you do one thing this month: Take a break.

♌ LEO A change to your work life could see you exploring a whole different area of interest this month. Speak up if it isn't what you want right now.

If you do one thing this month: Share your feelings.

♍ VIRGO You might know your worth on the inside but are you acting like you do on the outside? 'No' really is a complete sentence this Libra season.

If you do one thing this month: Stand your ground.

♎ **LIBRA** Take a look at how far you've come this birthday season – and don't stop moving for anyone. Your transformation is an inspiration to others for all the right reasons, Libra.

If you do one thing this month: Stick at it.

♏ **SCORPIO** Someone who cares about you enough to keep a secret may be about to become a bigger part of your life. They say 'don't look back, you're not going that way', but on this occasion, maybe you are?

If you do one thing this month: Give someone a (second?) chance.

♐ **SAGITTARIUS** Reconnecting with people you met during a work project or social event last year could reignite an old passion this month. Is it time to give a long-held dream another shot?

If you do one thing this month: Try again.

♑ **CAPRICORN** This is the big one, Capricorn. Your instincts were right all along! Magic – and money – await you. Enjoy celebrating your success.

If you do one thing this month: Big yourself up.

♒ **AQUARIUS** Take some time out this month, preferably somewhere sunny, and you'll soon find the headspace you need to make a big life decision. It's onwards and upwards for you this Libra season.

If you do one thing this month: Trust your gut.

♓ **PISCES** Say 'Yes' to something that scares you this Libra season because the reward will be worth it. Think life goals achieved and dreams come true. You did it, Pisces.

If you do one thing this month: Step into a new world.

OCTOBER

Key Cosmic Dates

NEW MOON ECLIPSE IN LIBRA *2 October*	The final eclipse of the year and a new moon in Libra offers magical insight into the relationships that matter the most (see p184–5).
JUPITER RETROGRADE BEGINS *9 October*	Expect a period of introspection, growth and deep thinking as the planet of fortune takes a backspin in communicative Gemini. Take a step back and reassess your plans (see p125).
PLUTO RETROGRADE ENDS *12 October*	If you spent the summer dealing with some big life stuff, Pluto direct might feel like the energy shift you need. Transformation awaits with the dwarf planet back in forward motion.
MERCURY ENTERS SCORPIO *13 October*	The messenger planet's spin in mysterious Scorpio reminds us that not all communication is overt. Trust your intuition.
FULL MOON IN ARIES *17 October*	If you can't remember the last time you put yourself first, the full super moon in Aries is here to remind you that you are the main character in your own life.
VENUS ENTERS SAGITTARIUS *17 October*	Love planet Venus in adventurous Sagittarius brings expansive vibes to our relationships. If you're ready to take a leap of faith with someone you love, the time might be right.
SCORPIO SEASON BEGINS *22 October*	Personal transformation, intimacy and connection all fall into focus with the sun in Scorpio. Be brave enough to go after what you want most and the rest should follow.
SAMHAIN *31 October*	Connect with your ancestors on the most magical night of the year.

RETROGRADE (RX) PLANETS

JUPITER RX
9 October–
4 February 2025
in Gemini

URANUS RX
1 September–
30 January 2025
in Taurus

NEPTUNE RX
2 July–7 December
in Pisces

SATURN RX
29 June–
15 November
in Pisces

PLUTO RX
2 May–12 October
(2 May–2 September
in Aquarius;
2 September–12 October
in Capricorn)

Wednesday
2
October
2024

NEW MOON ECLIPSE IN LIBRA

London 19:49 | New York 14:49 |
Los Angeles 11:49 | Tokyo 03:49 3 October |
Sydney 04:49 3 October

This month's new moon eclipse in Libra – the last eclipse of 2024 – could bring change, revelations and new beginnings in our most significant relationships. It's often best to sit back and see what comes up for you during an eclipse rather than try to force yourself into a shiny new list of intentions. Watch, wait and pay attention to the people who make life feel magical for you.

ECLIPSE SEASON

NEW MOON ECLIPSE REVEALS FOR YOUR SIGN

Take a break from intention setting this new moon

ARIES	♈	The best way to move forwards in a relationship is about to become obvious.
TAURUS	♉	Learn to put yourself first and others will follow suit.
GEMINI	♊	If you're waiting for a sign that now's the time to make a move, you may be about to get one.
CANCER	♋	Someone who feels like home is more interested than you realize.
LEO	♌	Words spoken now have magical meaning.
VIRGO	♍	An idea you have this eclipse could soon turn to gold.
LIBRA	♎	You'll soon know what needs to go to create space for magic in your life.
SCORPIO	♏	A spiritual guide or off-beat idea could help you find a new path.
SAGITTARIUS	♐	Invest time in people who make you feel more alive.
CAPRICORN	♑	The partnership needed for a key life goal is closer than you think.
AQUARIUS	♒	Unexpected travel plans may start a life-changing journey.
PISCES	♓	When you understand how you got here, you'll know exactly where you're going.

Thursday
17
October
2024

FULL MOON IN ARIES

London 12:26 | New York 07:26 | Los Angeles 04:26 | Tokyo 20:26 | Sydney 22:26

An Aries full super Hunter Moon brings themes of purpose and self-empowerment to the cosmic surface, urging us to believe in ourselves and our potential. What's stopping you from going after a big dream? Why can't you live the life you want to live? What do you need to help facilitate a bold step forwards? Now is the ideal time to shed self-doubt and begin to prioritize 'Project You'.

FULL MOON THEMES & QUESTIONS FOR YOUR SIGN

	THEMES	ASK YOURSELF
ARIES ♈	Starting over with an important personal project, realizing what you need to let go of in order to move forwards, doing something just for you	*What steps can I take now towards the future I dream of?*
TAURUS ♉	Dealing with a big wake-up call regarding your health or lifestyle choices, finding solace in spirituality, facing up to your past so you can move forwards	*How can I prioritize myself more?*
GEMINI ♊	Finding friends who love you just as you are, feeling part of something special, leaving an old community or group behind as you grow and evolve	*Who stands by me no matter what is happening in my life?*
CANCER ♋	Feeling inspired to change careers or follow a dream, knowing your worth, aiming higher, making space in your life to pursue a goal	*What's holding me back right now?*

Attune to the magic of the Aries full moon

	THEMES	ASK YOURSELF
LEO ♌	Planning a trip that means a lot to you, heading back into education to study something you find fascinating, being honest with yourself and others, finding something to believe in	*How can I spend more time doing the things that inspire me?*
VIRGO ♍	Changing your life, undergoing a personal transformation, discovering the truth about something, revealing a secret desire, receiving a surprise windfall	*How can I feel free to be my true self?*
LIBRA ♎	Finding love, making connections, bagging a business partner, team member or agent, feeling more supported in your home life, creating beauty in your world	*Why do I find it difficult to ask for help?*
SCORPIO ♏	Shaking things up, working hard on a project, putting your health and wellbeing first, starting a fitness journey, leaving an unhealthy habit behind	*How can I find balance in my life?*
SAGITTARIUS ♐	Stepping into the spotlight, enjoying life, celebrating, finding creative success, getting and enjoying lots of attention, feeling excited about what's to come	*How can I create more time for the things I enjoy?*
CAPRICORN ♑	Creating stability in your life, letting go of toxic people, feeling emotional, deciding on a permanent place to call home, spending time with family	*What do I need to prioritize now?*
AQUARIUS ♒	Talking it out, telling someone the truth, spending time writing or journalling, being asked to share your story, reconnecting with a sibling, finding new places to explore in your local area	*Which of my ideas needs my focus the most?*
PISCES ♓	Cashing in, accepting a pay out, getting a promotion, signing a deal, finding freedom, investing in yourself, seeing the potential in a project, feeling valued	*How can I believe in myself more?*

NOVEMBER

SCORPIO SEASON

♏

Welcome to Scorpio Season 190
Scorpio 191
Tune in to Scorpio Season 192
Starstruck: Wintering 193
Scorpio Season for Your Sign 194
Key Cosmic Dates 196
New Moon in Scorpio 198
Full Moon in Taurus 200

WELCOME TO SCORPIO SEASON

Lock eyes with Scorpio across a crowded room and it'll feel like they can see right into your soul. And don't even think about looking away. Intense, mysterious and magnetic, there's something about this water sign that draws people in and keeps them there. Scorpio is enigmatic, intuitive and captivating. Allow yourself to be pulled into Scorpio's world and you'll find yourself forever surrounded by magic. This sign has more power in one perfectly manicured finger than the rest of us can hope to know in a lifetime.

A born influencer, Scorpio doesn't have to try hard to convince people to do their bidding. In fact, they don't try at all. Scorpio can spot a trend years before it goes mainstream and has an uncanny knack for knowing what other people think, feel and need. There's nothing fake or forced about the way they live their lives, Scorpio does Scorpio and the universe delivers. This sign is a force to be reckoned with in the boardroom, the bedroom and everywhere in between.

Scorpio's focus and determination can sometimes come across as harsh and uncompromising but don't be fooled by first impressions. The real action happens beneath the surface with this sign. Emotions run high in Scorpio world and small talk is an anathema. Bring on the deep and meaningful conversations if you want access to the scorpion's inner sanctum. And once you're in, don't expect to leave easily. Scorpio can be jealous and possessive over the connections they care about but make peace with that and you'll always have someone you can trust with your darkest secrets.

The most psychic sign of the zodiac, Scorpio often finds solace in the mystical world. Take them on a haunted house tour or ask them to read your tarot cards and you'll be right on their spooky wavelength. Just don't expect that wavelength to stay the same for long. Above all else Scorpio is a master of transformation. Constantly changing and evolving, life is a magical joy ride with Scorpio at the wheel.

SCORPIO

22 October–20 November

THE MAGNET - *Mysterious. Intuitive. Enigmatic. Intense.*

SYMBOL	Scorpion
RULED BY	Pluto and Mars (co-ruler)
ELEMENT	Water
MODALITY	Fixed
RULES THE	8th House of Taboos, Power, Rebirth, Death & Inheritance
LUCKY DAY	Tuesday
STAR STONE	Labradorite
SOUL FLOWER	Peony
AT THEIR BEST	Brave, loyal, focused, charismatic
AT THEIR WORST	Guarded, possessive, manipulative, jealous
TAROT CARD	Death

SCORPIO 101

VIBE	Enigmatic with presence, purpose and magical powers
STYLE	Sleek lines, elevated classics, black with everything, statement dresses, up-and-coming labels, luxury fabrics, designer bags, leopard as a neutral
LOVES	Deep and meaningful conversations
HATES	Taking orders from anyone
MOST LIKELY TO	Help you dispose of a body
JUST DON'T	Distract them from their latest obsession
FIND THEM	Dancing in a dive bar, deep in conversation, casting spells, consulting the stars, starting from scratch, shortcutting through a graveyard, becoming a member of the board
BORN TO	Lead a coven

TUNE IN TO SCORPIO SEASON

Dive deep into November

REINVENT YOURSELF Fancy launching a fabulous new version of yourself into the world this month? Scorpio season is the perfect time to do it. Themes of transformation and rebirth abound when the sun meets the scorpion.

GET FOCUSED Obsessions, conspiracies and time-consuming tumbles down research rabbit holes come with the territory for Scorpio. Turn some of the scorpion's razor sharp focus towards a project you care about and witness the season's energy in action.

TRUST YOUR INTUITION As one of the most psychic signs of the zodiac, Scorpio is naturally tuned in and intuitive. Why not see what happens when you begin to trust your own intuition this month? Energy doesn't lie.

SEDUCE OR BE SEDUCED Play with fire, blow caution to the wind or embrace a lost weekend between the sheets. The sexiest sign of the zodiac brings seriously seductive vibes to a bedroom near you this month.

EMBRACE THE MYSTICAL If you've been waiting for the perfect time to learn tarot, connect with the moon or join a coven, that time is now. Magic, witchcraft and all things occult make perfect sense in Scorpio season.

KEEP SOMETHING TO YOURSELF Not everything has to be loudly announced on social media. Secretive Scorpio knows the power of holding something back, whether that's a love affair, new addition or passion project.

GO TO THE DARK SIDE Scorpio doesn't do toxic positivity. If you only do one thing this Scorpio season, allow yourself to feel all your feelings, especially the negative ones. Scorpio knows that there really is no light without darkness.

WINTERING

As 2024 draws to a close, the temptation to double down on goals set earlier in the year can become all-consuming. Weren't you meant to have read forty-eight books by now? And reorganized your wardrobe? And started a side hustle? And... stop right there. We can all learn something from nature's wisdom as the nights draw in this winter. Take it slow on the productivity panic, allow yourself to embrace the darkness and discover the magic that happens when you sink into the space inbetween.

LEARN TO LOVE WINTER

Rest and retreat as the nights draw in

LIGHT UP YOUR LIFE

String the fairylights early, change the bulbs in your table lamps and stop saving candles for best. Embracing the darkness of winter is all about finding light where you can. Try drinking your morning coffee by candlelight, moonbathing or hunkering down by a real fire.

CREATE A HAVEN

Turn a home into a haven with throws, blankets, cushions and multiple layered rugs. Invest in an array of aromatic hot drinks and turn those nights in on the sofa into an indulgent treat.

PRIORITIZE REST

Don't fall into the trap of thinking you need to be productive at all times. Take some time out to do absolutely nothing but relax and recline this winter, and discover where your mind wanders when you set it free.

GET OUTSIDE

Make the most of the daylight we do have with a bracing winter stroll, cup of tea in the garden or a few deep breaths on the doorstep. Pay attention to the world around you as the season changes.

WATCH THE SUNRISE

Darker mornings make watching the sunrise a breeze. Take a moment to witness the sky change from dark to light, even if the sun is missing in action.

SCORPIO SEASON FOR YOUR SIGN

♈ ARIES It's time to find your focus, Aries, and go all in until you get where you want to be. Say goodbye to self-sabotage for good.

If you do one thing this month: Trust your intuition.

♉ TAURUS A clandestine attraction could rock your world this month. Take care of your heart if you decide to dive in.

If you do one thing this month: Indulge.

♊ GEMINI Get your health in check before the festive season and you'll have plenty to celebrate by the end of the year. Remember small steps can become big steps that change your life.

If you do one thing this month: Step outside your comfort zone.

♋ CANCER Hate being the centre of attention? You might not get a choice in the matter this Scorpio season, Cancer. There's a spotlight with your name on it and it's time for you to shine.

If you do one thing this month: Rise up.

♌ LEO Remember when all you wanted is exactly what you have now? Celebrate how far you've come while you make even bigger plans for the future this month.

If you do one thing this month: Share the love.

♍ VIRGO A problem shared really is a problem halved for you this month. Ask for help - even though it's hard - and you'll soon be back on track.

If you do one thing this month: Talk it through.

♎ LIBRA Expect magic to find you this Scorpio season and it almost certainly will. This is set to be a month full of good news for your finances and future.

If you do one thing this month: Accept an offer.

♏ SCORPIO It's time to show the world what you're made of, Scorpio – and this time, hold nothing back. Your reinvention has begun.

If you do one thing this month: Take the compliment.

♐ SAGITTARIUS You've spent long enough looking outside yourself for answers, Sagittarius – it's time to look within. A retreat, meditation practice or inspiring read could change your outlook on life this month.

If you do one thing this month: Take some alone time.

♑ CAPRICORN A party or celebration could see you making an exciting new connection this Scorpio season. Spoiler: it's the quiet ones you need to watch.

If you do one thing this month: Send the email.

♒ AQUARIUS It's time to shake things up, sort yourself out and go for gold in your career, Aquarius. Your potential is so much greater than you give yourself credit for. You've got this.

If you do one thing this month: Apply yourself.

♓ PISCES Celebrate your success with a big trip somewhere magical and you'll soon be inspired all over again. It's time to enjoy the freedom your hard work has bought you.

If you do one thing this month: Go on an adventure.

NOVEMBER

Key Cosmic Dates

NEW MOON IN SCORPIO
1 November
A new moon in Scorpio is the perfect time to consider the ways in which we wish to transform our lives.

MERCURY ENTERS SAGITTARIUS
2 November
Spontaneous plans, open-ended conversations and trips into the unknown all look lit while the messenger planet takes a spin in Sagittarius.

MARS ENTERS LEO
4 November
Go-getting Mars in big-hearted Leo brings the right kind of energy to love affairs, passion projects and creative endeavours this month.

VENUS ENTERS CAPRICORN
11 November
Commitment, stability and tradition rule the roost while romantic Venus is in ambitious Capricorn. Power-couple vibes for the win.

FULL MOON IN TAURUS
15 November
Self-care and self-worth are big Taurus full moon themes. Consider what you might need to let go of to make space for more of both.

SATURN RETROGRADE ENDS
15 November
This long-awaited energy shift offers an opportunity to apply lessons learned over the past few months to our lives going forwards.

PLUTO RE-ENTERS AQUARIUS
19 November
With the planet of transformation back in Aquarius, it's a good time to refer to p42–5.

SAGITTARIUS SEASON BEGINS
21 November
Bring on the party vibes! Sagittarius season brings the fire and adventure to the end of 2024, urging us all to go out on a high.

MERCURY RETROGRADE BEGINS
26 November
Misunderstandings can play havoc with our friendships while communicative Mercury is retrograde in honest Sagittarius. Think before you tell someone those home truths!

RETROGRADE (RX) PLANETS

URANUS RX
1 September–
30 January 2025
in Taurus

JUPITER RX
9 October–
4 February 2025
in Gemini

MERCURY RX
26 November–
15 December
in Sagittarius

SATURN RX
29 June–
15 November
in Pisces

NEPTUNE RX
2 July–7 December
in Pisces

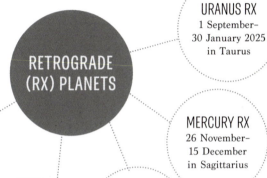

FRIDAY
1
November
2024

NEW MOON IN SCORPIO

London 12:47 | New York 08:47 | Los Angeles 05:47 | Tokyo 21:47 | Sydney 23:47

Themes of transformation and rebirth abound when the moon is new in Scorpio. This is the perfect time to renew your focus on what matters to you most right now and to consider if there's a part of you that remains hidden for all the wrong reasons. Know you have the power to be your truest self this new moon.

NEW MOON INTENTIONS FOR YOUR SIGN

Become who you really are

ARIES	♈	Focus your attention on the things you desire most.
TAURUS	♉	Speak up instead of expecting a partner to read your mind.
GEMINI	♊	Take a step towards the change you know you need to make on the path to health and happiness.
CANCER	♋	Allow your own hopes and dreams to take priority.
LEO	♌	Take responsibility for your own role in a tricky family situation.
VIRGO	♍	Announce an ambition or goal to keep you accountable.
LIBRA	♎	Refuse to accept less than you deserve.
SCORPIO	♏	Start over in life, love or creative endeavours.
SAGITTARIUS	♐	Forgive so you can begin to move forwards.
CAPRICORN	♑	Spend more time with people who love you as you are.
AQUARIUS	♒	Allow yourself to dream bigger when it comes to your career.
PISCES	♓	Start planning your next big adventure.

Friday
15
November
2024

FULL MOON IN TAURUS

London 21:28 | New York 16:28 | Los Angeles 13:28 | Tokyo 06:28 16 November | Sydney 08:28 16 November

Pleasure rules with a full Beaver Moon in Taurus so slow down, settle in and celebrate how far you've come with good food, good vibes and a long lie-in this weekend. Taurus teaches us to play the long game so make that your focus as you tune in to the power of this moon. What might you need to let go of to make more space for the finer things in life? How can you indulge yourself more? It's time to up the self-worth and believe in better.

FULL MOON THEMES & QUESTIONS FOR YOUR SIGN

	THEMES	ASK YOURSELF
ARIES ♈	Looking after yourself, investing in little luxuries, making time for relaxation, being rewarded for a job well done, making future plans	*What would I love to make happen in my life now?*
TAURUS ♉	Becoming the person you know you were born to be, taking more time over your appearance, finding a sense of purpose	*Who do I want by my side for the next stage of my life?*
GEMINI ♊	Seeking closure on a past hurt, forgiving someone, starting over, choosing yourself, practising yoga or meditation, believing a dream can come true	*What am I ready to release from my life?*
CANCER ♋	Meeting new people, feeling valued, supporting a cause, facing up to the truth about a friendship that's run its course, networking, feeling free	*Which connections do I value the most in my life?*

Attune to the magic of the Taurus full moon

	THEMES	ASK YOURSELF
LEO ♌	Making progress with a project, creating a five-year plan, finding success somewhere unexpected, earning more money, winning something	*How can I find more balance in my life?*
VIRGO ♍	Travelling for pleasure, choosing adventure, refusing to stay stuck, spending time outdoors, feeling excited about the future, learning a new skill	*What truly lights me up?*
LIBRA ♎	Finding a focus, falling in lust, changing your outlook, exploring the mystical world, receiving financial support, indulging yourself, facing an ending	*What have my biggest challenges taught me?*
SCORPIO ♏	Falling in love, making time for romance, wining and dining someone, choosing to commit, saying 'Yes', teaming up, loving yourself more	*How can I make more time for a relationship I don't want to lose?*
SAGITTARIUS ♐	Working hard, changing your daily routine, getting up earlier, feeling inspired, eating good food, getting more sleep	*If health is wealth, how rich am I?*
CAPRICORN ♑	Feeling inspired, spending time on a creative project, quitting the day job, finding an audience, inspiring others, having fun, hosting a celebration	*How do I want to remember this time in my life?*
AQUARIUS ♒	Moving house, creating more space in your life, making something beautiful, starting a family, feeling secure or wanting to feel more secure, settling down	*What does home mean to me now?*
PISCES ♓	Sharing your story, speaking in public, finding your voice, writing for fun, talking something through, being honest with yourself and others, trusting your instincts	*Am I sharing my vulnerable side with the right people?*

DECEMBER

SAGITTARIUS SEASON

Welcome to Sagittarius Season 204
Sagittarius 205
Tune in to Sagittarius Season 206
Starstruck: Winter Solstice 207
Sagittarius Season for Your Sign 208
Key Cosmic Dates 210
New Moon in Sagittarius 212
Full Moon in Gemini 214
Black Moon Magic 216

WELCOME TO SAGITTARIUS SEASON

It makes perfect sense for Sagittarius to preside over office party season and the festive build up. There's not much this fire sign likes more than throwing caution - and work deadlines - to the wind in favour of spontaneous fun. Determined to squeeze whatever joy they can out of life, optimism, adventure and festival spirit come with the territory for this magical sign. And honestly - because Sagittarius is big on honesty - you either love them or hate them for it.

Hanging out with the archer can feel exhausting for those who prefer routine and predictability. Travel, learning and new experiences are what make Sagittarius tick, which is great fun when they're whisking you to Paris for the weekend but a bit much when they arrive at your birthday party two days late because they found a warehouse party on the way. To love Sagittarius is to embrace their wild side - crazy schemes and one-way tickets included.

It's not all passport stamps and panic packing, though. The other side to Sagittarius is a constant thirst for knowledge. The zodiac's philosopher loves discovering new concepts and ideas on their quest for purpose and meaning. Sagittarius loves a physical journey but for them, life is a journey too. Believers, manifestors and early adopters, it pays to listen to what Sagittarius says because in a couple of years time everyone else will be saying the same thing.

The reckless side of Sagittarius means they're no stranger to failure or mistakes, which makes them down-to-earth mentors and teachers. Collecting experiences and tales to tell is the inspiration Sagittarius needs to keep going when the going gets tough. With Sagittarius what you see is what you get. They really are that lucky! That excitable! That determined to be the last one standing on a big night out!

Honest to a fault, you'll always know where you are with this sign and whether that's a good thing or a bad thing depends on how amenable you are to the truth - or, the truth according to Sagittarius at least. Learning to love the archer's blunt moments might feel like a challenge but the flipside is more than worth it. Amazing things happen with Sagittarius running the show.

SAGITTARIUS

21 November–20 December

THE WANDERER - *Adventurous. Inspiring. Honest. Spontaneous.*

SYMBOL	Archer
RULED BY	Jupiter
ELEMENT	Fire
MODALITY	Mutable
RULES THE	9th House of Philosophy, Higher Education, Travel, Religion & Publishing
LUCKY DAY	Thursday
STAR STONE	Turquoise
SOUL FLOWER	Dandelion clock
AT THEIR BEST	Optimistic, curious, self-assured, unique
AT THEIR WORST	Blunt, unfocused, unreliable, reckless
TAROT CARD	Temperance

SAGITTARIUS 101

VIBE	Globe-trotting adventurer determined to get the most out of life
STYLE	Bohemian vibes, statement pieces, festival wellies, sequins for daywear, high-low mix ups, travel trinkets, fancy dress
LOVES	Travel, adventure and new experiences
HATES	Feeling trapped
MOST LIKELY TO	Disappear in the dead of night leaving no new address
JUST DON'T	Ever confiscate their passport
FIND THEM	Running through an airport, hosting an after party, waking up in a field, taking notes in a lecture, at a manifestation workshop, running away from their problems
BORN TO	Roam

TUNE IN TO SAGITTARIUS SEASON

Make life an adventure

TAKE A TRIP There's not much Sagittarius finds more thrilling than a great escape. Even if hopping on the next plane to paradise isn't an option for you right now, allow yourself to think bigger when it comes to travel and adventure this Sagittarius season. Make the plan! Book the trip! Or simply explore the area you live in!

LOOK ON THE BRIGHT SIDE You can't keep Sagittarius down for long! Allow Sagittarius's optimistic spirit to sweep you away on a river of good vibes this season. Your luck is in and better days are coming – just as soon as you start believing!

GO BACK TO SCHOOL Learning is a lifelong affair for Sagittarius, who's forever signing up to courses and workshops or taking personal deep dives into the subjects that fascinate them. Ask yourself what truly piques your interest and make the time to learn more this season.

BE SPONTANEOUS Nothing changes if nothing changes and this adventurous sign refuses to stick with the status quo. Monday night clubbing? Lunch break fitness class? New route home? Say 'Yes' where you normally say 'No' and see where the cosmos takes you this season.

FIND SOMETHING TO BELIEVE IN Make some magic, seek solace in nature, embrace your spiritual side or find yourself a guru. Sagittarius loves a quest for truth, meaning and connected shared experience.

SPEAK YOUR TRUTH Honesty is always the best policy in Sagittarius world, to the point of being brutal at times. Now is a great time to practise speaking up for yourself; tell someone how you feel or share your voice with the world.

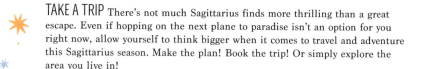

WINTER SOLSTICE

21 December

Six months on from the summer solstice and it's time to mark Yule's shortest day and longest night. Presided over by solid and reliable Capricorn, the winter solstice might be a time for quiet contemplation and hunkering down but it's also a celebration of returning light. From 21 December onwards every day becomes slightly longer than the next, so while there's plenty of winter left, the promise of brighter days ahead is within grasping distance.

CELEBRATE THE WINTER SOLSTICE

Return to light

GO CANDLELIT

Winter solstice celebrates the return to light but there's something magical about spending the longest night in the dark. Soak up the spirit of the season by turning off the television and pretending electricity hasn't been invented yet. Light as many candles as you can get your hands on and feel the magic.

FEED THE BIRDS

Spare a thought for the sparrows as the nights draw in and food sources become scarce. Fill a bird feeder, hang apples from a garden fence or create a smorgasbord of wildlife-friendly snacks.

GET CREATIVE

Make a door wreath, decorate a Yule log or gather festive foliage to decorate your house. Bringing the outside in is a brilliant way to celebrate nature and the changing seasons.

LOOK UP

Wrap up and get outside to experience the true wonder of winter. Take the time to watch the sun rise or set on the shortest day and gaze at the solstice night sky.

MAKE A WISH

Take some time to reflect on everything that's come to pass in the year so far and set intentions for the new one to come. Whisper your wishes for 2025 into the night sky, write them down by candelight or scrawl them in the sky with a sparkler.

SAGITTARIUS SEASON FOR YOUR SIGN

♈ **ARIES** Time spent reflecting on what 2024 has taught you and what you want to learn in 2025 will be time well spent this month. Midmonth travel plans look lit.

If you do one thing this month: Think bigger.

♉ **TAURUS** Take a step back before you get in too deep with something you don't really have the headspace for. Expect to find the focus you need as Sagittarius season draws to a close.

If you do one thing this month: Take care.

♊ **GEMINI** Love wins this December when you use lessons from the past to improve life in the here and now. It's time to level up in a relationship.

If you do one thing this month: Commit.

♋ **CANCER** Take some time out as Sagittarius season begins and by midmonth you'll be ready to hit the ground running on an exciting new project.

If you do one thing this month: Stay on track.

♌ **LEO** Allow yourself the space to shine this month. A project or person you took a chance on is about to show you how right you were to do so. You'll have plenty to celebrate as Sagittarius season comes to an end.

If you do one thing this month: Enjoy the attention.

♍ **VIRGO** Set clear boundaries in a tricky family situation this month and you'll soon see a better path forwards. You really can live life on your own terms if you want to, Virgo.

If you do one thing this month: Stand your ground.

♎ **LIBRA** Say what you mean and mean what you say this Sagittarius season, especially while Mercury remains retrograde. A misunderstanding could rock your boat this month.

If you do one thing this month: Be clear.

♏ **SCORPIO** A cash injection you were counting on could be subject to a frustrating delay as Sagittarius season begins but don't despair – your big moment is still coming and you'll be ending 2024 in style.

If you do one thing this month: Have patience.

♐ **SAGITTARIUS** A slower than usual start to birthday season might seem annoying at first but the magic that awaits is more than worth it. Be ready to hit upon your best idea yet.

If you do one thing this month: Plan a celebration of YOU.

♑ **CAPRICORN** Take some time out before life takes you down, Capricorn. Get away from it all this Sagittarius season and you'll soon be back on track and ready to nail it in the New Year.

If you do one thing this month: Relax.

♒ **AQUARIUS** Get out there and do what you do best this festive season: gather a crowd, turn up the volume and get the party started. A break from the grind is long overdue.

If you do one thing this month: Network.

♓ **PISCES** Don't let party season distract you from taking the next big step in your career. By the end of Sagittarius season you could have a very exciting offer on the table.

If you do one thing this month: Believe in a dream come true.

DECEMBER

Key Cosmic Dates

NEW MOON IN SAGITTARIUS
1 December

Think big this new moon and embrace the adventurous spirit of Sagittarius. Where do you want to go? What do you want to learn? How can you make your life feel even more full of potential?

MARS RETROGRADE BEGINS
6 December

The good times may not roll quite how you hoped they would while Mars is retrograde in Leo. Embrace a slower pace this party season and don't stress if your mojo feels missing in action (see p125 for tips on handling this).

VENUS ENTERS AQUARIUS
7 December

Lighten up and let love in while Venus is in free-spirited Aquarius. Venus in Aquarius is open-minded, forward-thinking and creative.

NEPTUNE RETROGRADE ENDS
7 December

Believing in a dream come true becomes easier with Neptune direct. Allow your imagination to run wild and enjoy the feeling that anything is possible.

FULL MOON IN GEMINI
15 December

Sharing your truth might feel like a priority with the full moon in chatty Gemini. If you're ready to move on from the past and be honest about your future, the time is now.

MERCURY RETROGRADE ENDS
15 December

Messenger Mercury stations direct, in time to put a rocket under party season. Make the most of a fresh burst of energy and action.

CAPRICORN SEASON BEGINS
21 December

Ambitious, reliable Capricorn arrives to take us through the festive main event and into the New Year. Use this cosmic handover to stand firm in your goals for the future.

WINTER SOLSTICE
21 December

The longest night invites us to embrace the darkness as the wheel of the year turns.

NEW MOON IN CAPRICORN
30 December

The second of two new moons this month, this black moon in Capricorn offers powerful manifesting potential right when we need it most. See p216–17.

RETROGRADE (RX) PLANETS

JUPITER RX
9 October–
4 February 2025
in Gemini

URANUS RX
1 September–
30 January 2025
in Taurus

MARS RX
6 December–
24 February 2025
(6 December–6 January
2025 in Leo)

MERCURY RX
26 November–
15 December
in Sagittarius

NEPTUNE RX
2 July–7 December
in Pisces

Sunday
1
December
2024

NEW MOON IN SAGITTARIUS

London 06:21 | New York 01:21 | Los Angeles 22:21 30 November | Tokyo 15:21 | Sydney 17:21

Make life feel more magical than ever by setting some adventurous intentions this new moon. A new moon in Sagittarius sprinkles the right kind of fairy dust on travel plans, education and new experiences – just don't expect anything to really get off the ground until Mercury stations direct midmonth.

NEW MOON INTENTIONS FOR YOUR SIGN

Expand your mind, expand your life

ARIES	♈	Hatch a travel plan that makes you feel alive.
TAURUS	♉	Make time for learning about something you find fascinating.
GEMINI	♊	Don't let distance get in the way of an amazing connection.
CANCER	♋	Find magic in the mundane and make your day-to-day life an adventure.
LEO	♌	Find a creative solution to an old problem and finally make the break.
VIRGO	♍	Be honest with those closest to you about what you need to thrive right now.
LIBRA	♎	Start sharing the story you know you were born to tell.
SCORPIO	♏	Put yourself first and don't settle for less this time.
SAGITTARIUS	♐	Make the change you know you need to make to move forwards.
CAPRICORN	♑	Start taking your work-life balance seriously.
AQUARIUS	♒	Surround yourself with people who make you feel good about yourself.
PISCES	♓	Trust that your big idea has the power to change your life.

Sunday
15
December
2024

FULL MOON IN GEMINI

London 09:01 | New York 04:01 |
Los Angeles 01:01 | Tokyo 18:01 |
Sydney 20:01

Expect big feelings and even bigger conversations this full Cold Moon, which occurs in communication-focused Gemini (on the same day that messenger planet Mercury ends its latest retrograde). If there's something you need to leave in the past where it belongs, this is the ideal moon to take a stand, move forwards and ask others to help you in your mission.

FULL MOON THEMES & QUESTIONS FOR YOUR SIGN

	THEME	ASK YOURSELF
ARIES ♈	Telling it like it is, standing up for yourself and others, letting rip with the home truths, feeling free to be yourself, releasing shame, being more vulnerable	*Who do I need to ask for help?*
TAURUS ♉	Getting a pay rise, seeing an investment come good, treating yourself, allowing yourself to indulge, talking to someone who can change your life, investing in your future	*How can I shift my mindset to create even more abundance?*
GEMINI ♊	Finally feeling free to move on, changing your outlook on life, reinventing yourself, changing your appearance, feeling confident, saying goodbye to the old you	*If failure was impossible what would I do next?*
CANCER ♋	Taking time out, committing to a spiritual practice, finding balance, forgiving someone, getting more sleep, finding peace in meditation	*How can I make rest a bigger feature in my life?*

Attune to the magic of the Gemini full moon

	THEME	ASK YOURSELF
LEO ♌	Meeting new people, feeling connected to a new group of people, sharing a vision, doing good for others, finding freedom, starting something new	*Who inspires me and why?*
VIRGO ♍	Getting an amazing job offer, branching out on your own, starting a business, finding an audience, feeling inspired, knowing your worth, receiving an award or bonus	*Why do I struggle to believe I deserve good things?*
LIBRA ♎	Starting a course, planning a trip, investing in books or learning, exploring new directions, practising a language, bonding with someone intriguing	*What do I no longer wish to put off in my life?*
SCORPIO ♏	Receiving a windfall, sharing a secret, flirtatious DMs, finding someone irresistible, making mistakes, picking yourself up and starting over, becoming who you really are	*How has this year changed me?*
SAGITTARIUS ♐	Making a commitment, falling in love, finding a cheerleader, teaming up in business, feeling supported	*Who will I still be in touch with in five years' time?*
CAPRICORN ♑	Taking a break, changing your work set-up, hitting the gym, eating better, finding balance in your life, taking small steps towards a big goal	*What do I want to do more of in 2025?*
AQUARIUS ♒	Finding fame, being the centre of attention, spending time with young people, getting more creative, attracting admirers, feeling confident, having fun	*How can I become even more authentic?*
PISCES ♓	Feeling at home, changing your family set-up, looking at houses, investing in interior design, choosing love, starting again, making yourself more comfortable right where you are	*How can I prioritize the people I love most?*

BLACK MOON MAGIC

MONDAY
30
December
2024

NEW MOON IN CAPRICORN

London 22:27 | New York 17:27 | Los Angeles 14:27 | Tokyo 07:27 31 December | Sydney 09:27 31 December

Known as a black moon, a second new moon in a calendar month offers a potent opportunity to double down on our intention setting. And what could be more perfectly timed than a black moon in ambitious Capricorn just before New Year? Use the power of this new moon to make a vision board, dream big and tune in to what you really want to call in to your life in 2025.

NEW MOON INTENTIONS FOR YOUR SIGN

The sky's the limit

ARIES	♈	Think even bigger when it comes to your career.
TAURUS	♉	Make a long-held travel dream happen.
GEMINI	♊	Make more time for intimacy in your life.
CANCER	♋	Level up in a relationship you know can go the distance.
LEO	♌	Change your daily routine to change your life.
VIRGO	♍	Make more time for the things you enjoy most.
LIBRA	♎	Find somewhere you can really call home.
SCORPIO	♏	Share your story to set yourself free.
SAGITTARIUS	♐	Know your worth and then double down.
CAPRICORN	♑	Recommit to a forgotten personal goal.
AQUARIUS	♒	Take the time you need to heal.
PISCES	♓	Trust that others are ready to help you level up.

DIVE DEEPER

The year might be over but if you're looking for more...

Degrees, aspects, transits, moon phases, planets, planets that aren't planets, sceptics, believers and everyone in between... talk about information overload! Astrology is a huge topic and one it's easy to feel excluded from. We've kept things as straightforward, accessible and entertaining as possible throughout this almanac so that anyone can use it, regardless of their level of astro knowledge. That doesn't mean there isn't a whole universe of additional insights available if you want them, though. If you feel like you're only just getting started, read on for more detail.

THE HOUSES

We've focused primarily on the signs and the planets here but the twelve astrological houses are another important part of the cosmic picture. In your birth chart, each house represents a different area of your life and may host one or more planets depending on how the sky looked when you made your Earth debut.

You can glean a lot from knowing that your Uranus sign is in Sagittarius - big up the 1981–88 babies switching up the narrative on work, travel and spirituality - but knowing what house this planet falls in adds a layer of personal insight and understanding.

Getting to grips with the symbolism of the houses and how they relate to different areas of life is a great way to up your cosmic knowledge.

Not every house in your chart will have planets in it.

1ST HOUSE
Self, Image, Identity & Personality
First impressions, personal appearance, public identity, what we reveal about ourselves to others, how we wish to be seen.

2ND HOUSE
Wealth, Values & Possessions
The things we value in life (personal and material), our approach to finances, possessions and ability to mobilize resources.

3RD HOUSE
Communication
Communication, the mind, learning, how we connect with other people, siblings, local travel.

4TH HOUSE

Home, Family & Domesticity
The domestic sphere, home and family, mothers and motherhood, our need for stability, security, comfort and emotional support.

5TH HOUSE

Fun, Fame, Creativity, Romance & Children
Creativity, good times, fun, romance and the role children play in our lives. Joy, play, flirtation and fame are also 5th House themes.

6TH HOUSE

Daily Routines, Health, Wellbeing & Hard Work
The days of our lives play out in the 6th House. It offers insights into our routines, work, health, wellbeing and our capacity to get a job done.

7TH HOUSE

Love, Romance, Relationships & Duos
Relationships, partnerships (of all kinds), love lives and ability to connect with others.

8TH HOUSE

Transformation, Taboos, Power, Rebirth, Death & Inheritance
Taboos, secrets, sex, death, transformations of all kinds and other people's money.

9TH HOUSE

Philosophy, Higher Education, Travel, Religion & Publishing
Activity in this expansive house can show us how education, travel and learning might play out in our lives.

10TH HOUSE

Career & Success
10th House themes include tradition, status, power, authority, fathers and fatherhood and power couples.

11TH HOUSE

Friendship & Community
Friends, social skills, networking, community spirit and innovation. Planets here may indicate idealism, humanitarian values or a thirst for freedom.

12TH HOUSE

Endings, Spirituality & the Subconscious
Our connection to the spiritual world lies in the 12th House, which offers insights into our hopes, dreams, imagination, closure and healing.

MOON PHASES

We've mentioned the new and full moon throughout this almanac but there's a lot more to the phases of the moon than that. Learning to understand moon phases more fully can be a brilliant way to manage your energy levels and accept the inevitable ebb and flow of life.

We've based our moon images on the northern hemisphere. If you're in the southern hemisphere the moon's illumination is seen from the opposite angle.

NEW MOON

Fresh starts and intention setting

The start of the moon cycle is the ideal time to make plans and set intentions for the months ahead. The moon isn't visible in the sky at this stage so it's also the best time to gaze at the stars.

WAXING MOON

Taking action and making progress

As the moon grows in visible illumination the time is right for us to take steps towards putting our plans into action. What begins as a tiny sliver of crescent moon (make a wish when you see it a few days after the new moon) gradually becomes brighter and brighter until...

FULL MOON

Manifesting magic and letting go

The full moon occurs around fourteen days after the new moon, bringing magic, manifestation and big feelings to light. You don't have to be mystically minded to feel the effects of a full moon but it's a great time to invite a bit of cosmic magic into your life and – because it's also the very beginning of the moon's waning phase – let go of anything that's no longer serving you.

WANING MOON

Reassessing and slowing down

The moon's slowly waning illumination is a reminder that we don't have to be on it and productive all the time. The waning moon phase is a good time to take stock and adjust your plans as we work our way back to the beginning of the cycle.

ASPECTS

To keep things beginner friendly we haven't referenced planetary aspects often in this almanac, but they offer a world of insight should you wish to learn more.

CONJUNCTION A conjunction occurs when two planets are close to each other in the sky, creating an amplifying - and usually harmonious - alliance.

OPPOSITION Oppositions occur when two planets are opposite each other in the sky, creating what is often an air of tension.

SEXTILE A sextile is typically - but not always - a good-vibes aspect that occurs when planets are separated by two astrological signs.

SQUARE Astro squares - when planets are 90 degrees apart, often bring conflict and tension.

TRINE A dreamy aspect that occurs when planets are four signs apart - bringing good vibes and harmony.

MORE, MORE, MORE

To keep things simple we've stuck to talking about the main planets throughout this book but there's plenty more to discover in your chart if you have an appetite for more.

CHIRON Initially classified as an asteroid and now as a minor planet, Chiron is known as the wounded healer. Its placement in your chart can show where your deepest need for healing is.

LUNAR NODES The South Node and North Node reveal our destiny in life. The North Node shows what we're here to learn, while the South Node reveals insights into what we already know, our karmic comfort zone.

THE ASTRO AXIS If you've reached this page in this book you likely already know and understand your rising sign or ascendant. This is one of four powerful lines in your chart that can reveal magical insights into who you are and what you're here to do. Forming a big cross through your chart (look for the abbreviations AC, DC, MC and IC) these lines reveal our public selves (ascendant), how we relate to others (descendant), our purpose or legacy in life (midheaven) and our roots and foundations (imum coeli).

ABOUT THE AUTHOR

Emma Howarth is a lifestyle and travel writer, horoscope columnist for *Glamour* and the author of *A Year Of Mystical Thinking: Make Life Feel Magical Again*, a memoir about the year she spent exploring different spiritual practices in a bid to make life better.

Emma spent five years as an editor at *Time Out*, where she worked on titles including *London for Londoners*, *Parties* and *The Little Black Book of London* as well as guides to Tokyo and Paris, among others. She was contributing editor at *Smallish* and her work has appeared in publications including *Red*, *Psychologies*, *Metro*, *The Telegraph*, *Project Calm* and *Soul & Spirit*.

Obsessed with astrology since she first found out she was a Pisces (aged seven!), Emma likes nothing more than gazing at the stars. She writes about astrology for *Glamour* and on Instagram @emmahowarthwrites. She lives on the edge of Kent and East Sussex with her husband, two daughters and a cat called Moonbeam.
www.emmahowarth.com

ABOUT THE ILLUSTRATOR

Katarina Samohin is an illustrator based in Belgrade, Serbia. She began her journey into the world of illustration at the beginning of 2020, after one lovely trip to Amsterdam. Her art is inspired by nature, dreams and small everyday things that bring joy to life. Her illustrations reflect her soul – they are a kind of illustrated journal. As a quiet person, drawing helps her to express herself and open up to the world. Her sketchbook or iPad are always in her bag wherever she goes. Katarina likes to collect illustrated books and she enjoys sunsets, a beautiful spring day and the cherry blossom season, which is her favourite part of the year.

ACKNOWLEDGEMENTS

Many stars must align for a book like this to make its way into the world and I thank my lucky ones that Chloe Murphy, Virgo extraordinaire, dreamed up this almanac and asked me to bring it to life. Massive thanks also to Katerina Menhennet, Hanri van Wyk and everyone at Leaping Hare for being such a dream team. And to Katarina Samohin whose illustrations bring these pages to life.

Thanks also to my agent Oscar Janson-Smith, my editors at *Glamour* Bianca London and Ali Pantony, and astrologer Bex Milford (@cosmic_cures) whose eagle eyes made the perfect second pair for this book. I'm also forever grateful to my brilliant on and offline astrology friends Lucy Porter (@lucy.porter.portal) and Alice Bell (@stalkalice), whose astute insights make star-gazing cooler, cleverer and more inspiring every day.

Thanks to Fred Espenak and Sumit Dutta whose NASA Sky Events Calendar I used to double-check moon times. And cosmic high fives to my almanac writing tea break colleagues Steve Cook, Conor Hamilton and sky-dwellers Steve and Ray Lucas, who must have heard the words 'I'm trying to write a book' a thousand times as they asked me to make decisions about paint and leaking roofs.

Writing about astrology is the best job ever and my biggest inspirations are always the friends and family whose lives pop into my head when I think about their sign... I started a list of you all and then got worried everyone would take it the wrong way (especially the Aries crowd - yes, you got a mention and, of course, your name was first!) so instead I'm going to end with a big-up to my favourite Leo, Aquarius and fellow Piscean - Alexis, Cleo and Lola. Can't think of three better people to spin around the sun with.

Leaping Hare Press

First published in 2023 by Leaping Hare Press
an imprint of The Quarto Group.
One Triptych Place, London, SE1 9SH
United Kingdom
T (0)20 7700 6700
www.QuartoKnows.com

A catalogue record for this book is available from the British Library.

ISBN 978-0-7112-8634-4
Ebook ISBN 978-0-7112-8635-1

10 9 8 7 6 5 4 3 2 1

Design by Hanri van Wyk

Printed in China

The information in this book is for informational purposes only and is not intended as a guide to replace the advice of a counsellor, physician or medical practitioner. There is the possibility of allergic or other adverse reactions from the use of any ingredients, essential oils or other items mentioned in this book. You should seek the advice of your doctor or other qualified health provider with any questions you may have, especially if you have a medical condition or are pregnant. The authors, editors and publisher make no representations or warranties with respect to the accuracy, completeness, fitness for a particular purpose or currency of the contents of this book and exclude all liability to the extent permitted by law for any errors or omissions and for any injury, illness, loss, damage, liability or expense (whether direct or indirect) from the use or application of any of the information contained in this book.